WISDOM LITERATURE

VERY REV. PETER SAMUEL KUCER, MSA

En Route Books and Media, LLC

St. Louis, MO

⚓ENROUTE
Make the time

En Route Books and Media, LLC
5705 Rhodes Avenue
St. Louis, MO 63109

Cover credit: TJ Burdick

Library of Congress Control Number: 2020944870

ISBN-13: 978-1-952464-29-4

Acknowledgments

I would particularly like to acknowledge Very Rev. Edward Przygocki, M.S.A., U.S.A., Province Provincial of the Missionaries of the Holy Apostles, who gave me permission to publish.

Special thanks also to Dr. Sebastian Mahfood, O.P., President of En Route Books and Media, for publishing this work.

Contents

Introduction

As explained by Bergsma and Pitre, Wisdom Literature's order follows a noticeable historical logic. Books that are at least associated with earlier times come first. For this reason, Job is first since it more closely resembles

---

[1] Photograph: Myrabella [Public domain], "Apse mosaic of the Virgin and Child," https://commons.wikimedia.org/wiki/File:Apse_mosaic_Hagia_Sophia_Virgin_and_Child.jpg.

the preceding historical books than the other Wisdom books. Job's similarities to the historical books include lengthy narrative dimensions, and some textual indications that the events in Job take place after Noah and before Moses since although the flood is referred to in Job (Job 22:16) Moses is not, observes Mark Copeland.[2]

Job is followed by the Psalms since the Psalms are associated with King David who comes significantly after Moses. Four books attributed to King David's son, Solomon, then follow: Proverbs, Ecclesiastes, Song of Solomon, and Wisdom. The books of Wisdom then conclude with Sirach, a book written in the second century B.C.

Reflecting the title of one of the books, all seven books teach wisdom, which is a practical type of knowledge that is to be reflected in right living. In quoting Oswald Chambers, Mark Copeland pithily writes that Job teaches "How to suffer;" Psalms teaches "How to pray;" Proverbs teaches "How to act;" Ecclesiastes teaches "How to enjoy;" and the Song of Solomon teaches, "How to love."[3] We can add that Sirach teaches how to suffer, pray, act, enjoy and love in fear of God which is the "beginning of wisdom (Sirach 1:14 *RSVCE*)."[4]

An obvious difference between the historical books and the books of Wisdom is that the historical books narrate history while the Wisdom books are essentially poetic. Another difference that is less immediately apparent is the emphasis on the universal in the books of Wisdom. In contrast, while the rest of the Old Testament contains universality, the universal elements in Wisdom Literature, such as Israel's role as "first-born son" who is to lead all nations to God (Exodus 4:22 *RSVCE*), are repeatedly contextualized by particularity: specific people, specific land,

---

[2] Mark Copeland, "The Book of Job," ccel.org, http://www.ccel.org/contrib/exec outlines/job/job 01.htm.

[3] Copeland, "The Book of Job."

[4] John Bergsma and Brant Pitre, *A Catholic Introduction to the Bible, Volume I* (San Francisco: Ignatius Press, 2018), 533.

and specific laws unique to a chosen people. This difference is highlighted, comments Fr. Joseph Alobaidi, by the distinction between the Mosaic Covenant given on Mount Sinai from the Davidic Covenant given on Mount Zion. The latter covenant, the Davidic covenant, is associated with the books of Wisdom.[5]

Due to the need of Israel to be purified from its attachment to idolatrous practices acquired during their Egyptian captivity and learned from surrounding pagan nations, God, Pitre explains, separated the Israelites from the rest of the nations. God separated the Israelites to best prepare them for the time when they would be called to fulfill their role as the "first-born son (Exodus 4:22)" who leads all nations to the worship of the true God.[6] The time of separation and purification entailed following laws that distinguished the Israelites from pagan nations, and living under a covenant that was understood as primarily between Israel and God and not so much between God and all nations. This type of covenantal relationship is evident in how God introduces the Ten Commandments. God does so by addressing the particular nation of Israel, "I am the Lord your God, who brought you out of the land of Egypt (Exodus 20:2 *RSVCE*)." This is not intended, as evident in other passages, to be understood as a covenant exclusively with Israel in such a way that it only applies to Israel. After all, Israel retains the role to be the elder brother to the other nations. However, not until the time is right in salvation history will God intensify the universal demands for the Chosen People of Israel.

God chooses the time of King David to intensify the universal mission to all people that Israel had by being the elder brother, the elder nation chosen for the sake of the many nations. God fulfills his salvific plan by establishing a covenant with David that is, as Alobaidi explains, inter-

---

[5] Joseph Alobaidi, class notes and lectures on *Wisdom Literature* (Washington, D.C.: Dominican House of Studies, Spring Semester 2008).

[6] Brant Pitre, *Genesis and the Books of Moses: Unlocking the Mysteries of the Pentateuch,* MP 3, 13, 19.

national, inclusive, and whose place of worship is not a movable tabernacle guarded by a nation of tribes but rather a Temple that all people, from all nations can visit to worship.[7] The Wisdom Literature associated with King David and King Solomon reflects this universal calling of Israel. The books of Wisdom do so by teaching wisdom that is applicable to all, in terminology that is seldom particular. Even the main character of the first book of Wisdom, Job, points out Alobaidi, "is not an Israelite [and] Jonah [(sometimes classified as Wisdom Literature)] spoke to the Ninevites who were not Israelites."[8] A similar occurrence, he adds, is in the book of Song of Songs which does not identify the main young man and young woman of the Song of Songs.[9] The reason for this deliberate lack of particularity is so that Israel's universal chosen role from the beginning (Matthew 19:8 *RSVCE*) of being a light to all nations as first-born son is brought to the fore.

Benedict XVI attributes much of the distinguishing universal aspects within the biblical Wisdom Literature to Israel's providential engagement with other nations during Israel's Babylonian Captivity and after the captivity. The first influence is Babylonian. This is followed by Egyptian influence and then by Greek influence.

Israel's geographical location in West Asia is a main reason why North African, Asian and European cultures intersect in Israel as is particularly evident in Wisdom Literature. As Benedict XVI states, " 'interculturality' is part of the original shape of Christianity" which builds upon the interculturality of the Old Testament.[10] Consequently, both the Old and New Testaments reflect this interculturality as "a real synthesis of cultures

---

[7] Alobaidi, class notes and lectures.

[8] Alobaidi, class notes and lectures.

[9] Alobaidi, class notes and lectures.

[10] Joseph Cardinal Ratzinger, *Truth and Tolerance: Christian Belief and World Religions*, trans. H. Taylor (San Francisco: Ignatius Press, 2004), 85.

…[and] not simply the expression of the culture of the people of Israel."[11] God's Revelation through Israel, the synthesis of cultures (Asian, African, and European) is a way that Israel, explains Benedict XVI, transcended its own culture "into the wide-open spaces of truth that is common to all" as a universal faith.

The transcendent faith revealed to Israel began with Abraham who left the land of Ur, modern day Iraq, for Canaan, modern day Israel, and,

---

[11] Ratzinger, *Truth and Tolerance*, 198-200.

[12] "Western Asia," Wikimedia. Identified as "Free to share and use commercially." https://commons.wikimedia.org/wiki/File:Middle_east.jpg.

defines Benedict XVI, is a "struggle of faith against what is Israel's own."[13] "This faith," Benedict XVI writes:

> is in continual opposition to Israel's own religious inclinations and to its own religious culture, which is inclined to express itself in the cult of high places, in worship of the queen of heaven, and in the claims to power of its own kingdom. From the anger of God and of Moses against the worship of the golden calf on Sinai, right down to the late postexilic prophets, it is always a matter of tearing Israel out of its cultural identity, contrary to its own religious wishes, so that it has, so to speak, to leave off the worship of its own nationality, the cult of "blood and soil," to bow down before the wholly other, the God who is not their own, who has created heaven and earth and who is the God of all peoples.[14]

The New Testament in the person of Jesus brings the movement within the Old Testament towards a universal faith to completion. Due to his conversion in meeting Jesus, St. Paul further applies Jesus' fulfillment of Israel's faith by his, writes Benedict XVI:

> struggle to break out from the limits of the law…[St. Paul] takes this fundamental movement of the Old Testament to its logical goal. This signifies the complete universalizing of the faith, which is freed from being proper to the social order of a particular people. All peoples are now invited to participate in this process of transcending their own heritage that first began in Israel; they are invited to turn to the God who, for his part, transcended his own limits in Jesus Christ, who has broken down "the dividing wall of hostility" between us (Eph 2:14) and in the self-deprivation of the Cross has led us toward one another.

---

[13] Ratzinger, *Truth and Tolerance*, 198-200.
[14] Ratzinger, *Truth and Tolerance*, 198-200.

Faith in Jesus Christ is, therefore, of its nature, a continual opening of oneself, God's action of breaking into the human world and in response to this man's breaking out toward God, which at the same time leads men toward one another. Everything anyone possesses now belongs to everyone, and everything else becomes at the same time our own, this whole comprehended in the Father's words to the elder son: "All that is mine is yours" (Lk 15:31), which returns again in the high-priestly prayer of Jesus, as the Son addresses the Father: "All mine are thine, and thine are mine" (Jn 17:10)."[15]

Biblical Wisdom Literature functions "as a kind of 'bridge,'" comment Bergsma and Pitre, "between the Old and New Testament," between the gradual universalizing movement of the Old Testament and the fulfillment of this universalization of Israel's belief in the person of Jesus.[16] The various cultures that intersect in Israel help to free Israel from an excessively nationalistic understanding of God. In this freeing process, Israel developed its Wisdom Literature.

As explained by Alobaidi, while lacking a word for Wisdom, the Babylonians did have an understanding of a "wise" person whose "wisdom" is defined by an acquired, refined skill due to experience at perfecting a craft. Proverbs similarly defines Wisdom in this manner, "the wise man...the man of understanding acquire skill (Proverbs 1:5 RSVCE)." However, according to Proverbs, the essential skill that qualifies a person in being wise is excellence in living. As Proverbs states, he who finds wisdom, "finds life...but he who misses me injures himself; all who hate me love death (Proverbs 8:35 RSVCE)." Echoing this definition of wisdom as excellence in living, the letter of James asks, "Who is wise and understanding among you? By his good life let him show his works in the

---

[15] Ratzinger, *Truth and Tolerance*, 198-200.

[16] Bergsma and Pitre, *A Catholic Introduction to the Bible, Volume I,* Kindle location, 15001.

meekness of wisdom (James 3:13 *RSVCE*)."

The Egyptians, writes Alobaidi, "exercised a more decision influence" on Biblical Wisdom Literature than the Babylonians did. They did so with their concept of *Maat*. *Maat* refers to right order between "heaven and earth." Right order between heaven and earth is achieved by the practice of truth and justice. The visible fruit of this order is harmony, is peace.[17]

Greek thought contributed yet another dimension to Wisdom Literature. According to Benedict XVI, after profiting from Egyptian wisdom, Biblical Wisdom Literature "shows more and more evidence of contact with Greek thought."[18] Due to contact with Greek philosophy and its rigorous logic, writes Benedict XVI, "faith in a single God is developed and given greater depth, and … [as t]he meaning of monotheism is further elucidated, and, associated with an attempt to understand the world in rational fashion, it becomes more rationally persuasive."[19] In contrast to pagan origin myths, which teach that chaos is most essential to reality, and is the cause of all, including reason, Wisdom Literature clearly affirms that the world is capable of being rationally understood because it is created by a reasonable God who wisdom was "before the beginning of the earth (Proverbs 8:23 *RSVCE*)."

Since God is not only, as Benedict XVI emphasizes, "originating reason," but also is holy, morally holy, we are commanded to "consecrate yourselves therefore, and be holy, for I am holy (Leviticus 11:44 *RSVCE*)." By conceiving "of the world" writes Benedict XVI, "as reflecting the rationality of the Creator" Wisdom Literature relates the order of the world with the order of human beings, in other words, "of understanding the world with morality, because wisdom, which builds up matter and the world, is at the same time a moral wisdom, which expresses essential

---

[17] Alobaidi, class notes and lectures.

[18] Ratzinger, *Truth and Tolerance*, 149.

[19] Ratzinger, *Truth and Tolerance*, 150.

guidelines for living."[20] This leads the books of Wisdom to present "[t]he whole of the Torah, Israel's law for living... as wisdom's self-portrait, as the translation of wisdom into human language and human instruction."[21]

The transformation of Jewish belief expressed in the Old Testament into a more readily accessible language for all people due to contact with Greek culture and Greek culture's emphasis, especially by Socrates and Plato, on reason was intensified, adds Benedict XVI, when in the 4th century B.C. Jewish people took up residence in Alexandria, Egypt during the Ptolemaic Greek empire. The following century, the Hebrew Bible was translated into Greek, according to tradition, by 70 scholars. In Genesis chapter eleven, the number 70 represents the number of nations in the world. The universal dimension that the number 70 represents, writes Benedict XVI, "may signify that with this translation the Old Testament moved beyond Israel, reaching out to all the peoples of the earth."[22]

The Septuagint translation offered to the people of the vast Greek Empire a type of wisdom, especially in Biblical Wisdom Literature, that is not reducible to the Babylonian concept of technical knowledge that one perfects through experience. Instead, as stated previously, Biblical Wisdom offers universal values, and truths on how to live life with excellence, with moral perfection. According to Biblical Wisdom, we are called to holiness since we are created in the image and likeness of God who is holy. We are, therefore, to reflect divine holiness and in so doing will experience ever great peace as we live more and more in accordance with our created natures.

Our present age with its exaltation of scientific, technical knowledge is similar to the Babylonian's absence of even a word for wisdom, as presented in Wisdom Literature. "If" comments Benedict XVI:

---

[20] Ratzinger, *Truth and Tolerance*, 149.

[21] Ratzinger, *Truth and Tolerance*, 149.

[22] Ratzinger, *Truth and Tolerance*, 152-153.

only scientific knowledge counts as knowledge ... then there are no universal values that are binding on all of us. And if that is the case, then there is no law except that which is called law at any given moment—the order imposed by those who have put themselves in power. There is then no qualitative difference between the power exercised in the name of the law and that exercised by him who breaks the law; the concept of a constitutional state becomes empty. That is our situation. ... by its exactness, exact knowledge bars the way to wisdom, which asks about the most profound depths of our existence.[23]

Wisdom Literature's teaching of a non-technical knowledge that is universally valid since it is concerned with right living for all people united knowledge with right living. In so doing, at the time of Jesus, comments Benedict XVI, wisdom was understood in "Rabbinic Judaism" as "very practical, very realistic" since it identified wisdom "with the knowledge and practice of the Torah."[24] This development prepared for the coming of Jesus, the Torah, the universal law in person, in the flesh, of "the pure and undiminished wisdom of God."[25]

As St. Paul explains, Jesus as law in the flesh, as law fulfilled in the Spirit, invites us to participate in his divine life and by so doing enables us to follow God's law, as principally expressed by the Ten Commandments, commandments that reflect how God has created us. Without participating in God's life offered to us by Jesus we cannot live up to the demands of our created natures that are created to follow moral law. In this way the written moral law can only condemn and not help us.

---

[23] Joseph Ratzinger, *Principles of Catholic Theology: Building Stones for a Fundamental Theology*, trans. M.F. McCarthy (San Francisco: Ignatius Press, 1987), 359-360.

[24] Ratzinger, *Principles of Catholic Theology*, 361-362.

[25] Ratzinger, *Principles of Catholic Theology*, 361-362.

Jesus as law in flesh, as fulfilled law in person who allows us to share in his divine life, though, not only indicates what we are to do by his life but also gives us the ability, the grace, a relationship with God to live in accordance with the law. "For the law of the Spirit of life in Christ Jesus has set me free from the law of sin and death. For God has done what the law, weakened by the flesh, could not do: sending his own Son in the likeness of sinful flesh and for sin, he condemned sin in the flesh, in order that the just requirement of the law might be fulfilled in us, who walk not according to the flesh but according to the Spirit (Romans 8:2-4 *RSVCE*)." As St. Paul clearly lays out, Jesus offers all the possibility of being set free from the law of sin and condemnation by the law. In this way Jesus is universal wisdom in the flesh whom all can learn from and rely on to live moral lives.

The universal dimension of wisdom in Wisdom Literature that prepares for the coming of wisdom in the flesh is specified in a number of complementary ways. As explained by Alobaidi these include wisdom as teaching, wisdom as learning, wisdom as morality, wisdom as reverence (fear), and wisdom as heavenly blessings.[26]

Those who teach others the various ways of wisdom ordinarily have acquired their wisdom by life experiences. This type of wisdom is often the wisdom of the older people since they have lived longer than the younger. As Job says to Zophar, "Wisdom is with the aged, and understanding in length of days (Job 12:12 *RSVCE*)." The wise can become wiser if they remain open to learning from others, "Give instruction to a wise man, and he will be still wiser (Proverbs 9:9 *RSVCE*)." Similarly, Proverbs teaches, "Hear instruction and be wise (Proverbs 8:33 *RSVCE*)"; "A wise son hears his father's instruction (Proverbs 13:1 *RSVCE*)"; "The way of a fool is right in his own eyes, but a wise man listens to advice (Proverbs 12:15 *RSVCE*)."

Proverbs, as other books of Wisdom, repeatedly teaches universal

---

[26] Alobaidi, class notes and lectures.

moral precepts that when followed indicate one is wise and when not followed indicate one is foolish, "A prudent man conceals his knowledge, but fools proclaim their folly (Proverbs 12:23 *RSVCE*)." Those who "turn away from evil" are described as possessing the wisdom of those who "fear the Lord (Proverbs 3:7 *RSVCE*)." So important is fear of the Lord that a few chapters later Proverbs asserts what it had similarly taught in its first chapter: "The fear of the Lord is the beginning of wisdom (Proverbs 9:10 *RSVCE*)." Fear of the Lord is related to God blessing those who are wise. "Fear God, and keep his commandments.... For God will bring every deed into judgment, with every secret thing, whether good or evil (Ecclesiastes 12:13-14 *RSVCE*)."

Section Questions

1. According to Bergsma and Pitre, how and why are Wisdom Literature ordered? Include the following in your response: Job, Psalms, Proverbs, Ecclesiastes, Song of Solomon, Wisdom, Sirach; Identify Which are Associated with David or Solomon; Explain Why Job is First.

2. As explained by Copeland, which phrases correspond to which books of Wisdom:

   Job, Sirach, Proverbs, Psalms, Song of Solomon, Ecclesiastes

   Living in Fear of God as "beginning of wisdom," "How to suffer," "How to act," "How to love," "How to pray," "How to enjoy"

3. Contrast the Historical Books with the Wisdom Books on particularity and universality. Include the following in your response: Mosaic Covenant, Davidic Covenant, Separation, National Emphasis, International Emphasis, Nationality of Job, Names of Man and Woman in Song of Songs.

4. How does Wisdom Literature synthesize and elevate Babylonian, Egyptian, and Greek teachings on wisdom? Include the following in your response: Hebrew Word for Wisdom, Practical Skill, *Maat*, Logos, Incarnation, New Testament.

Job

Introduction

The book of Job can be divided into four parts. The first two chapters introduces principle characters: Job, God, Satan, and Job's three friends. Chapters three through thirty-one present in poetic discourse a con-

---

[1] Gustave Doré [Public domain], "Gustave Doré, *Job Speaks with His Friends*," https://commons.wikimedia.org/wiki/File:119.Job_Speaks_with_His_Friends.jpg.

versation between Job and his friends: Eliphaz, Bildad, and Zophar. The third section, chapters thirty-two through thirty-seven contains the conversation between Job and the young man Elihu. The fourth section, chapters thirty-eight through forty-two concludes with God's response to Job. We will begin our reflection by focusing on the prologue.

First Part: Chapters 1 and 2

After briefly identifying Job as a God-fearing, non-Israelite from the land of "Uz (Job 1:1 *RSVCE*)," the prologue then describes God permitting Satan to test Job with suffering. The suffering is to test if Job will remain faithful to God or not. In agreeing to Job being tested, comments Miller, God demonstrates that God is concerned about human beings for God wants to preserve Job's reputation. Understood in this way the entire book of Job is, writes Miller, "about divine providence and human value" and less on why a good God permits a just, good man to suffer from evil.[2]

In the test, Job loses his property, his children, and his dignity. Also, ugly sores develop over his entire body. Despite these sufferings Job undergoes, Job does not reject God and Satan emerges as a loser. Victor P. Hamilton observes that the Hebrew word in Job for Satan (שָׂטָן), meaning adversary or accuser, is preceded by the definite article "the". According to Hamilton, "this indicates that 'the satan' is a title, not a personal name. Satan is not who he is, but what he is. He does not merit a name, and in antiquity, not to have a name was to be reduced to virtual nonexistence."[3]

---

[2] Robert D. Miller II, *Understanding the Old Testament* (Chantilly: The Teaching Company, 2019), 353. "Is this a comforting answer to 'Why do bad things happen to good people?' No. But I don't think this book is designed to comfort anyone. I often tell students that Job is not the book to give to a suffering friend. Instead, it's a magnificent literary parable about the place of the individual human being in the cosmos."

[3] Victor P. Hamilton, *Handbook on the Pentateuch, Second Edition* (Grand Rapids: Baker Academic, 2005), 40.

Since God "is Love," Benedict XVI writes, God "is not a being turned in on himself, without relations to other."[4] The Satan by being nameless, by being relationless, by lacking a personal name that indicates relation to others is diametrically opposed to God who as Trinity "is the act of relating." [5]

Since sin harms and sometimes even destroys relationships, such as can occur with adultery, by sinning human beings resemble Satan who is opposed to lasting relationships. Although opposed to God who is relation, one who is tempted to sin, like Job to reject even God (Job 2:9), is also tempted to be God, as the serpent in the garden tempted Adam and Eve with "you will be like God." However, as Benedict XVI points out, according to Revelation, principally in the person of Jesus Christ:

The One who is truly like God does not hold graspingly to his autonomy, to the limitlessness of his ability and his willing. He does the contrary: he becomes completely dependent, he becomes a slave. Because he does not go the route of power but that of love, he can descend into the depths of Adam's lie, into the depths of death, and there raise up truth and life. Thus, Christ is the new Adam, with whom humankind begins anew. The Son, who is by nature relationship and relatedness, reestablishes relationships. His arms, spread out on the cross, are an open invitation to relationship, which is continually offered to us. The cross, the place of his obedience, is the true tree of life.[6]

In further expounding on the lack of personhood of the devil due to

---

[4] Joseph Ratzinger, *Europe, Today and Tomorrow: Addressing the Fundamental Issues*, trans. J. Miller (San Francisco: Ignatius Press, 2007), 97-98.

[5] Benedict XVI, *Day by Day with Pope Benedict XVI*, ed. Peter John Cameron (San Francisco: Ignatius Press, 2006), 28.

[6] Benedict XVI, *Day by Day with Pope Benedict XVI*, 56.

his anti-relational identity, Benedict XVI writes, "If someone asks whether the devil is a person, we would probably have to answer more accurately that he is the Un-person, the disintegration and collapse of personhood, and that is why he characteristically appears without a face."[7] As a power who stands "between" God and the world, the devil in his desire to destroy relationship "'interferes' everywhere and obstructs unity."[8] The true "in between" power, states Benedict XVI, is the Holy Spirit who "is that 'in between' in which the Father and the Son are one as the one God; in the power of this 'in between', the Christian confronts that demonic 'in between'.[9]

These in between powers are not brought out in the Old Testament as they are in the New Testament "because," explains Benedict XVI:

> at first any ambiguity about faith in the one and only God had to be firmly opposed. In an environment saturated with idols, where the boundaries between good and bad gods were blurred, any mention of Satan would have detracted from the clarity of the decisive profession of faith. Only after the belief in the one God, with all its consequences, had become the unshakable possession of Israel could the view be widened to include powers that overrun the world of man, without letting them challenge God's uniqueness.[10]

The in between power of the Holy Spirit and the demonic in between power of *Ha Satanas* resemble each other but in this resemblance are essentially different. Both point out faults. The demonic does so by being an accuser that his name implies when used in the book of Job. In Hebrew,

---

[7] Benedict XVI, *Dogma and Preaching: Applying Christian Doctrine to Daily Life*, trans. Michael J. Miller (San Francisco: Ignatius Press, 2011), 204.

[8] Benedict XVI, *Dogma and Preaching*, 204.

[9] Benedict XVI, *Dogma and Preaching*, 204.

[10] Benedict XVI, *Dogma and Preaching*, 200-201.

the very name *satan*, explains Hahn, "is first of all a legal term for an 'accuser' or 'adversary.'"[11] The Holy Spirit also reveals sin by "convincing the world of sin (John 16:8 *RSVCE*)," but as a paraclete (παράκλητος), variably translated as helper, advocate, and consoler.[12] In contrast, with the demonic name *satan*, meaning a legal accuser, the word paraclete (παράκλητος) originates from a Greek word meaning, "a legal advocate."[13] The Holy Spirit convicts the world of sin (John 16:8), especially the sin of rejection and crucifying Christ, and is at the same time the consoler who offers hope in Christ's Resurrection from the dead.[14] Through his Resurrection Christ promises the fallen world purification and redemption.

---

[11] Scott Hahn, *Catholic Bible Dictionary* (New York: Doubleday, 2009), 816

[12] "3875. Paraklétos," biblehub.com, https://biblehub.com/greek/3875.htm.

[13] HELPS Word-studies, "3875. Paraklétos," biblehub.com, https://biblehub.com/greek/3875.htm.

[14] This idea is inspired by Benedict XVI but the source is as of yet unknown.

[15] Léon Bonnat [Public domain], "Léon Bonnat – Job," https://commons.wikimedia.org/wiki/File:L%C3%A9on_Bonnat_-_Job.jpg.

Section Questions

1. According to Miller why is the book of Job not so much on how God in his goodness can permit evil especially to good people and more on "Providence and Human Value"? In your response, define the terms you use carefully.

2. Why is the term Satan a title and not a personal name? In your response include the following: definite article the, personal name, title.

3. Compare and contrast Satan with the Holy Spirit. In your response include the following: Accusing, Convicting, Scattering, Uniting, anti-relationship, pro-relationship, in-between power.

Second Part: Chapters 3-31

As stated previously, the second section presents in poetic form a dialogue between Job and his friends. Chapter three opens with Job cursing "the day of his birth (Job 3:1 *RSVCE*)." He proceeds to ask many questions on why there is suffering. Eliphaz then responds by arguing suffering is a direct consequence of sin. He even asks "who that was innocent ever perished? Or where were the upright cut off? (Job 4:7 *RSVCE*)." In his response, Job describes in poetic verse his suffering while defending his innocence, "Is there any wrong on my tongue? (Job 6:30 *RSVCE*)" After stating his innocence Job qualifies it in a variety of way including, "Though I am innocent, I cannot answer Him…Though I am blameless, he would prove me perverse (Job 9:15, 20 *RSVCE*)."

Bildad follows Eliphaz by claiming that if Job amends his ways "surely then he will rouse himself for you and reward you for rightful habitation (Job 8:6 *RSVCE*)." Job retorts with, "But how can man be just before God? (Job 9:2 RSVCE)" Zophar follows by accusing Job of wrongdoing which merits punishment, "Know then that God exacts of you less than your guilt deserves (Job 11:6 *RSVCE*)." After Job responds, Eliphaz harshly reprimands Job, "you are doing away with the fear of God ... For iniquity teaches your mouth (Job 15:4-5 *RSVCE*)." Job once again maintains his innocence, "My face is red with weeping...although there is no violence in my hands, and my prayer is pure (Job 16:16-17 *RSVCE*)."

In the subsequent chapters through thirty-one, the three friends try to convince Job of his error in claiming to be innocent. Job defends his relative innocence while pointing out that contrary to their simplistic logic, in this life the wicked and not the good prosper, "Why do the wicked live, reach old age, and grow mighty in power? (Job 21:7 *RSVCE*)" Aware of this reality, Job appeals in hope to a "Redeemer" who will come to his rescue: "I know that my Redeemer lives, and at last he will stand upon the earth, and after my skin has been thus destroyed, then from my flesh I shall see God (Job 19:25-26 *RSVCE*)." From the perspective of Catholic faith, this hope of Job in the midst of his veering into despair, this hope of Job for someone to save him is fulfilled in Christ who ordinarily rescues us not from the difficulties of this unjust world, points out Rolheiser. Instead, Jesus redeems us a savior who suffers with us, who invites us to suffer with Him, so that our suffering united to Christ's perfect suffering becomes filled with meaning, with the meaning of redemption in Christ and salvation by dying and rising with Christ.[16]

Undeterred by Job's questions and expression of deep pain, his friends continue to defend the mistaken idea that in this life if you are good you

---

[16] Ron Rolheiser, "The Resurrection as Revealing God as Redeemer, not Rescuer," ronrolheiser.com, http://ronrolheiser.com/the-resurrection-as-revealing-god-as-redeemer-not-as-rescuer/#.Woy_CWa-Ki5.

will be blessed by God and if wicked punished. Eliphaz even intensifies his rebuke of Job by asking, "Is not your wickedness great (Job 21:5 *RSVCE*)?" Job responds by defending his innocence: "I have not departed from the commandment of his lips (Job 23:12 *RSVCE*)." The continued accusations Job faces cause him to examine his conscience (Job 31). Bergsma and Pitre observe that up to the coming of Christ this examination of conscience is unparalleled for its sensitivity. In anticipation of Christ, Job reflects on sins of omission, on the interior sinful desire against the sixth commandment that are consented to and do not necessarily involve any physical action, and on other interior sins such as pride, delighting in someone's misfortune, or envy, being sorrowful for someone's good. Job's sensitive conscience, write Bergsma and Pitre, "goes far beyond the requirements of the Mosaic law and will not be matched again in the canon until Jesus' exposition of the New Law in the Sermon on the Mount (Mt 5 – 7)."[17]

Section Questions

1. How does Eliphaz understand the relationship between suffering and sin and what is Job's response?

2. How does Rolheiser present Jesus as a redeemer (Job 19:25) and not so much as a rescuer?

3. According to Bergsma and Pitre, how does Job's sensitive conscience (Job 31) anticipate the New Testament?

---

[17] John Bergsma and Brant Pitre, *A Catholic Introduction to the Bible, Volume I* (San Francisco: Ignatius Press, 2018), 543.

Third Part: Chapters 32-37

In the third section, the young man Elihu responds in anger, "I am young in years, and you are aged; therefore, I was timid and afraid to declare my opinion to you (Job 32:6 *RSVCE*)." Elihu cautions Job from questioning God's justice and accuses Job of one "who goes in company with evildoers and walks with wicked men (Job 34:8 *RSVCE*)." Because of Job's wickedness, Elihu reasons, God has punished him, "For according to the work of a man he [God] will repay him and according to his ways he will make it befall him (Job 34:11 *RSVCE*)."

Fourth Part: Chapters 38-42

In the fourth section, God corrects Job and, near the end of the last

---

[18] Ilya Repin [Public domain], "*Job and His Friends* by Ilya Repin (1869)," https://commons.wikimedia.org/wiki/File:Job_and_his_friends.jpg.

chapter, rebukes Job's friends, "My wrath is kindled against you and against your two friends; for you have not spoken of me what is right, as my servant Job has (Job 42:10 *RSVCE*). God corrects Job, Miller comments, by asking Job a series of questions with the intention of helping Job to recognize that God's justice is not simply a matter of punishing the bad and rewarding the just, for God rains both on rich soil and upon deserts; God cares for gentle animals, ferocious animals, and dumb animals:

> Who has ... to bring rain on a land where no man is, on the desert in which there is no man ...? ... Can you hunt the prey for the lion, or satisfy the appetite of the young lions...? The wings of the ostrich wave proudly: but are they the pinions of plumage of love? For she leaves her eggs to the earth, and lets them be warmed on the ground, forgetting that a foot may crush them... (Job 38:26, 39 39:13-15 *RSVCE*).[19]

In chapter forty, God goes further, comments Miller, by telling Job that even the terrifying sea monster, Leviathan, is no match for God's power. Even though this sea serpent has a mouth out of which "sparks of fire leap forth" and nostrils out of which "comes forth smoke (Job 41:19, 21 *RSVCE*)," God has the ability to "play with him as with a bird" and place a "leash (Job 41:5 *RSVCE*)" on him.[20]

After aiding Job in the realization that God is all powerful and that God's justice is mysterious, by transcending this world's understanding of justice, God then not only miraculously heals Job but also restores Job's "fortunes... twice as much as he had before (Job 42:10 *RSVCE*)." As

---

[19] Robert D. Miller II, *Understanding the Old Testament* (Chantilly: The Teaching Company, 2019), 352.

[20] Miller, *Understanding the Old Testament*, 383.

Alobaidi points out, this ending "does not fit reality"[21] since very rarely, if ever, do those who suffer tragic losses regain their possessions, and relationships. Since the ending of Job does not match how life actually unfolds in almost all similar circumstances, contends Alobaidi, the book of Job points to a reality that goes beyond this earthly reality; it points to the heavenly dimension that although overlapping the earthly reality also transcends this world. Only when fully in the heavenly, other world reality will those who are innocent and just like Job be definitively embraced by God.[22]

The specific heavenly reality that acts as a bridge between this world and the heavenly world that the book of Job points to is Jesus Christ, for as true God and true Man Jesus serves as a bridge. As with all of reality, the book of Job is elevated and finds its fulfillment in Jesus Christ. Aspects where this is evident include the book's presentation of a just, suffering man who at the end of the book is rewarded in this life by Job's fortunes being restored "twice as much as he had before (Job 42:10 *RSVCE*)." Unlike Job, Christ, the perfectly just one, was not rewarded in this life; instead, he was crucified. Christ's crucifixion teaches that although the just may suffer in this life and may not experience any earthly reward, they are offered participation in the heavenly reality of Christ's life which will be only experienced in a definitive manner by dying and rising with Christ.

Another aspect that the Revelation of Jesus clarifies is the belief that although wisdom is a primordial reality, it is, nonetheless, created as Proverbs indicates: "The Lord created [or acquired] at the beginning of his work, the first of his acts of old. Ages ago I was set up, at the first, before the beginning of the earth (Proverbs 8:23 *RSVCE*)." Jesus in his human nature is created but not in his divine nature that is united to His human nature in the divine person of Jesus Christ. In disagreement with this basic

---

[21] Joseph Alobaidi, class notes and lectures on *Wisdom Literature* (Washington, D.C.: Dominican House of Studies, Spring Semester 2008).

[22] Alobaidi, class notes and lectures.

teaching of Christianity, the early heretical priest Arius (256-336) cited the passage from Proverbs among others as evidence that since the New Testament identifies Jesus as Wisdom, Jesus is, therefore, created and not equal to the Father. For this reason, comments Bergsma and Pitre, the Council of Nicaea (325) defined Christ as "begotten" by the Father and "not made" not created.[23]

Jesus as the uncreated Word of the Father who is eternally begotten in the Holy Spirit by the Father and not made affirms that loving truth is more essential than chaos, which the sea and its monsters (Rahab, sea

---

[23] Bergsma and Pitre, *A Catholic Introduction to the Bible, Volume I,* 615.

[24] Laurent de La Hyre [Public domain], "Job Restored to Prosperity by Laurent de La Hyre (1648)," https://commons.wikimedia.org/wiki/File:Job-restored-to-prosperity.jpg.

dragons, and Leviathan) represent: "In the beginning was the Word, and the Word was with God, and the Word was God (John 1:1 *RSVCE*)."[25]

Yet another way where Jesus, especially Jesus understood as the Word of the Father, fulfills the wisdom teaching in Job is in respect to the fourth section "where" as Alobaidi summarizes, "God says if you do not understand it is because you cannot understand."[26] In so doing, Jesus purifies all Wisdom Literature. He does so as the Incarnate Word who reveals that although God's ways are not man's ways as the Lord states clearly in Isaiah, "For my thoughts are not your thoughts, neither are you ways my ways (Isaiah 55:8 *RSVCE*)," it is also true that God's ways are not completely inaccessible, unknowable, and mysterious to human beings.

The discursive process and its associated categorical way of understanding reality will always fall short of knowing reality as it actually is, above all the foundation and cause of reality, God. As Lateran Council IV (1215), teaches, "For between creator and creature there can be noted no similarity so great that a greater dissimilarity cannot be seen between them."[27] As applied to our use of words, this means that all words, including theological terms, that aid human beings in understanding God always inadequately present God. However, at the same time this inadequacy is not a total inadequacy. There can be a similarity, with a greater difference, between theological words and God. In a similar vein of thought, Benedict XVI argues:

> But this infinite dissimilarity still does not turn knowledge into ignorance, truth into falsehood. It seems to me that we should turn this question about presumption the other way around: Is it not

---

[25] Alobaidi, class notes and lectures. Job 3:8, 7:12, 9:8, 9:13, 26:12-13, and 26:41, 41.

[26] Alobaidi, class notes and lectures.

[27] "Fourth Lateran Council: 1215, no. 2," papalencyclicals.net, https://www.papalencyclicals.net/councils/ecum12-2.htm.

presumption to say that God cannot give us the truth as a gift? That he cannot open our eyes? Does it not show contempt for God to say that, once we have been born blind, truth is not our concern? Is it not a degradation of man and of his longing for God to claim that we human beings are merely groping in the dark forever?[28]

Belief in Christ as the eternal Word of the Father strongly affirms that with respect to encountering God we are not completely blind, since God was revealed to us as Word who is knowable, but knowable by faith and not in a clear, distinct technical way after the manner of physical sciences. The mysteries of our faith, which invite humans in their entirety (intellect, will, emotions...),[29] are not mysteries that are completely devoid of reason as, points out Benedict XVI, were "many pagan mystery cults" that in focusing only on will, emotions, and desire led to the loss of reason in "intoxication." Instead, he adds, the mysteries of faith are "Logos-mysteries" which "lead to Logos, that is, to the creative reason on which the meaning of all things is based."[30]

Section Questions

1. According to Elihu why is Job punished? Include in your response the following: God, Justice, the Wicked.

2. In correcting Job's friends how does God refer to Job?

---

[28] Joseph Ratzinger, *On the Way to Jesus Christ*, trans. M.J. Miller (San Francisco: Ignatius Press, 2005), 69.

[29] Benedict XVI, *Day by Day with Pope Benedict XVI*, 25.

[30] Ratzinger, *On the Way to Jesus Christ*, 136.

3. In correcting Job, how does God broaden Job's understanding of divine justice and divine power? Include the following in your response: lions, ostriches, fields, deserts, Leviathan.

4. How does Jesus bring Job to fulfillment? Include the following in your response: Specifically Contrast End of Job's Life with End of Jesus's Death on the Cross, Jesus as Bridge, Divine Justice, Suffering of the Just.

5. According to Proverbs 8:23 wisdom is created. With respect to Jesus, how did Arius interpret this verse? How and why is Arius' teaching erroneous? Include the following in your response: Begotten, Created, Chaos, Leviathan, Most Essential Reality.

Psalms

Introduction

The word psalm comes from the Greek word *psalmos* (ψαλμός) which in turn is based on the Greek verb *psalló* meaning "to play, twitch, twang,

---

play, sing."[2] The Greek Septuagint Bible's plural title *psalmoi* for the book of Psalms indicates that the psalms are to be sung and even accompanied by a string, plucked musical instrument, especially a harp.[3] The Hebrew word for the Psalms similarly indicates the musical nature of the book. The Hebrew title is *Tehillim* (תְּהִלִּים), the plural form of *tehillah* (תְּהִלָּה) meaning "praise, song of praise."[4]

The 150 psalms are collected into five books: 1-41, 42-72, 73-89, 90-106, 106-150. As identified by Robert G. Bratcher and William D. Reyburn, the psalms contained in these five books are laments, hymns of praise, songs of thanksgiving, psalms of confidence, psalms on Zion, psalms of God as King, pilgrimage psalms, psalms of wisdom, liturgical psalms and a few psalms that are difficult to classify.[5]

One hundred and sixteen of the 150 psalms have a variety of titles. Although some are not yet translatable, many are. Certain titles that are not translatable, comments Miller, "indicate the type of composition" such as a *miktam* (מִכְתָּם) that is used to identify Psalms sixteen and fifty-six through sixty.[6] The titles that are translatable, explains Miller, are given for a number of reasons, including as melody indicators (Psalms 22, 57, 59, 80), as liturgical indicators (for example Psalms 30, 70, 100), for pilgrims to Jerusalem (Psalms of Ascent 120-134), for the leader (often translated choirmaster), for specific musical instruments (for example Psalms 4-6), and for a specific person (David, Sons of Korah, Asaph, Moses, Solomon, Ethan the Ezrahite).[7]

---

[2] "5567. Psalló," biblehub.com, https://biblehub.com/greek/5567.htm.

[3] "5568. Psalmos," biblehub.com, https://biblehub.com/greek/5568.htm.

[4] "8416. Tehillah," biblehub.com, https://biblehub.com/hebrew/8416.htm.

[5] R.G. Bratcher, and W.D. Reyburn, *A Translator's Handbook on the Book of Psalms* (New York: United Bible Societies, 1991), 3.

[6] "4387. Miktam," biblehub.com, https://biblehub.com/hebrew/4387.htm.

[7] Miller, *Understanding the Old Testament*, 307. Miller identifies 73 psalms that "are designated *le-David.* That could mean 'by David,' or 'for David," or 'dedicated to David.' Some of them, it clearly is intended to mean 'by David,'

The historical context that these titles provide is limited, points out Miller, since scholars from ancient times, notably Theodoret of Cyr, argued that the psalms predate the titles. This may explain historical inaccuracies in the titles.[8]

Transitioning to the individual psalms, the first and last psalm help to give meaning to the variety of psalms. According to Alobaidi, while Psalm 1 emphasizes man, "Blessed is the man (Psalm 1:1 *RSVCE)* the last psalm (150) is on praising God "Praise the Lord! (Psalm 150:1 *RSVCE)."* The first

---

because it tells you an event in David's life when he supposedly composed the psalm. It's because of this that we often speak of the Psalms being written by King David, the shepherd boy who becomes Israel's second king." Robert D. Miller II, *Understanding the Old Testament* (Chantilly: The Teaching Company, 2019), 307-308.

[8] Miller, *Understanding the Old Testament,* 308. "A number of times, the contents of a psalm, that is le-David, speaks of things that didn't exist in David's own time, especially the Temple of Jerusalem, which wasn't built until David's son Solomon. The temple appears in Psalm 3:4; 5:7; 18:6; 24:7-9; 28:2; 122:1. And in Psalm 51:18, we even get a prayer for the rebuilding of a destroyed Jerusalem, so this has to be from after the Babylonian conquest.

These anachronisms are not the only problem. Sometimes, the historical note in the title clashes with the account of the episode described in the historical books of the Old Testament. So, Psalm 34, in the title says, "When David feigned madness in the presence of Abimelech, who turned him out." Except that in the story of 1 Samuel 21:14, the guy isn't named Abimelech, he is named Achish.

The title of Psalm 90 is completely at odds with 2 Samuel 8:13 and 1 Chronicles 18:12. The psalm title says Joab defeated 12,000 men. The historical books have 18,000. Here, the victorious general is named Joab; in Samuel, it's David himself, and in the account in the book of Chronicles, it's someone named Abishai. But it's never Joab. ...

The titles ... group the Psalms into clusters. So there are four 'David' collections, four bunches of psalms that are le-David all together—almost: Psalms 3-41 (but not 10 and 33); 51-72 (but not 66-67, 71, 72); and what's interesting is that at the end of that unit we get 72:20: 'The Prayers of David, son of Jesse, are ended.' Except they aren't—there are two more David collections: 108-110 and 138-145."

psalm, consequently, states Alobaidi, "leads to the last psalm – God."[9] All psalms in between represent stages of our journey to God.

Returning to the first psalms, the first word of this psalm in Hebrew, is "Blessed," *ashrey* (אַשְׁרֵי), which is based on the Hebrew root "אָשַׁר", meaning "happiness, blessedness."[10] According to Alobaidi, Jewish oral tradition represented in the Talmud defines happiness as being with others and sadness as being alone. For this reason, he adds, when the word happiness is used in the Old Testament it is always plural, since by definition one cannot be happy alone.[11]

For the reason pointed out by Alobaidi, Jewish commentary on Genesis chapter two typically highlight the verse, "Then the Lord God said, 'It is not good that the man should be alone; I will make him a helper fit for him (Genesis 2:18 *RSVCE*).'" God then creates the first woman who by complementing Adam and not duplicating him is able to unite with him and bear life, thereby fulfilling the first Biblical commandment to Adam and Eve, "Be fruitful and multiply (Genesis 1:28 *RSVCE*)." In fulfilling this commandment, by bringing forth new life, Adam and Eve fulfill their social natures. In commenting on these verses, Rabbi Shmuel Goldin brings out the communitarian dimension of being human with:

> God creates Adam alone, as Adam needs to understand that his aloneness is not good. He needs to feel the emptiness caused by in his isolation. Only upon feeling that emptiness can he understand why it is necessary to share with another. Adam has to learn that the choice

---

[9] Alobaidi, class notes and lectures.

[10] "835. Esher," biblehub.com, https://biblehub.com/hebrew/835.htm.

[11] Alobaidi, class notes and lectures. "From 'ashar; happiness; only in masculine plural construction as interjection, how happy! -- blessed, happy." "835. esher," Strong's Exhaustive Condordance," biblehub.com, https://biblehub.com/hebrew/835.htm#:~:text=From%20%27ashar%3B%20happiness%3B%20only%20in%20masculine%20plural%20construction,how%20happy%21%20--%20blessed%2C%20happy.%20see%20HEBREW%20%27ashar.

for human relationships, with all of its consequent sacrifice and pain, is a better choice than the isolation that he now experiences. Had God created Chava immediately, Adam would have been unwilling to give of himself or of his world.[12]

God created Adam as an intrinsically social creature who lacks freedom to live in accordance with his social nature if he is alone. The reason man is created a relational, social creature is because, professes the Catholic faith, men and women are created in the image and likeness of God who is a Trinity of persons, a communion of persons. As stated by Benedict XVI God "is the relation of three Persons to one another"[13]; the Father relates by "being-for" the other two persons, the Son relates by "being-from" the Father in the love of the Holy Spirit and the Holy Spirit relates by "being-with" the Father and the Son.[14] Since freedom is a shared social reality a "coexistence of freedoms"[15] this means that in order for the social reality to be in harmony the persons who share this social reality must be ordered properly, principally to God and then to one another. For this reason, the Ten Commandments are "not," writes Benedict XVI, "the opposite pole to our freedom but are rather the concrete form it takes. They are … the foundation for every law of freedom and are the one truly liberating power in human history" for they "are the answer to the inner demands of our nature."[16]

The complementary relationship of a man and a woman in marriage

---

[12] Rabbi Shmuel Goldin, "Not Good for Man to Be Alone," ou.org, https://www.ou.org/torah/parsha/rabbi-goldin-on-parsha/not_good_for_man_to_be_alone/.

[13] Joseph Ratzinger, *Introduction to Christianity (Revised Edition)*, trans. J.R. Foster (San Francisco: Ignatius Press, 2004), 306.

[14] Joseph Cardinal Ratzinger, *Truth and Tolerance: Christian Belief and World Religions*, trans. H. Taylor (San Francisco: Ignatius Press, 2004), 248.

[15] Benedict XVI, *Day by Day with Pope Benedict XVI*, 96.

[16] Ratzinger, *Truth and Tolerance*, 254-255.

where each mutually supports the other and in so doing provides the context for the other to experience a deeper freedom to live in accordance with their social natures well demonstrates that the Biblical teaching that personal freedom is a shared social reality. To safeguard this freedom as a social reality, law, especially the Ten Commandments, are not, explains Benedict XVI, to be viewed as an "obstacle to freedom; rather, it constitutes freedom. The absence of law is the absence of freedom."[17] The essence of the Ten Commandments existed prior to their written since human beings are created by God with these laws inscribed in their nature.

Only by acting in accordance with how we are created, as social creatures whose freedom is be shared in co-existence with other people's freedom, will we experience rest, peace. Perceiving freedom as participation in the social reality of what it means to be a human person means also to acknowledge that we depend on others and only by depending on others, argues Benedict XVI, do we experience freedom in its fullness. As members of the mystical body of Christ we are to mutually help one another. Without the feet bringing the body to various places, the eyes lack freedom to exercise sight in diverse ways. The eyes depend on the feet to experience greater freedom in fulfilling its created nature.[18]

Beginning with the first psalm, the Psalms repeatedly teach that the happiness that we are created for is encountered in the context of community life. Only by being relational, loving others and not simply loving oneself, will we experience being "Blessed (Psalm 1:1 *RSVCE*)," happy.

Section Questions

1. Define *psalmos* and *tehillim* and then explain how they reveal the nature of the Psalms.

---

[17] Ratzinger, *Truth and Tolerance*, 247-249.
[18] Ratzinger, *Truth and Tolerance*, 247-249.

2. How many psalms are there, and how many books make up the Psalms?

3. List at least three classifications of psalms as identified by Bratcher and Reyburn.

4. List at least three people to whom some psalms are attributed.

5. Who is the primary subject of the first psalm and of the last psalm and what, according to Albaidi, does this indicate about the direction of the Psalms?

6. Psalm 1 begins with "Blessed is the man." According to Jewish oral tradition, as recorded in the Talmud, why is this Hebrew word Blessed or Happy always in the plural, and what does this mean with respect to true human freedom?

Praying the Psalms

The psalms have been and are a main source for corporate prayer in both Judaism and Catholicism. Corporate prayer in which the individuals pray the same words greatly helps to balance private prayer. In private prayer the individual has a marked tendency to pray according to what he is feeling and thinking. If these feelings and thoughts are expressed by words, the words will represent one person's subjective experiences. The tradition of praying the psalms together helps to prevent the tendency of individual prayer becoming excessively, writes Benedict XVI, "subjective and end[ing] up reflecting ourselves more than the living God."[19]

20

That the psalms are not strictly organized according to emotional content, such as all sorrowful psalms in one section and all songs of gratitude in another, further, writes Miller, helps to "cover the gamut of emotions. And it has the potential to keep people from being obsessively stuck in one psychological state."[21]

---

[19] Pope Benedict XVI, *Jesus of Nazareth, From the Baptism in the Jordan to the Transfiguration,* trans. Adrian J. Walker (New York: Double Day, 2007), Kindle location 1998 of 5265.

[20] Julius Schnorr von Carolsfeld [Public domain], "David is depicted giving a psalm to pray for deliverance in this 1860 woodcut by Julius Schnorr von Karolsfeld," https://commons.wikimedia.org/wiki/File:Schnorr_von_Carolsfeld_Bibel_in_Bildern_1860_136.png.

[21] Miller, *Understanding the Old Testament,* 323.

Praying the psalms liturgically helps to prevent an overly subjective kind of prayer that reflects individual human reality more than God. Corporate prayer of the psalms does so by, explains Benedict XVI, requiring those praying together to first say words before thinking and feeling. As a consequence, the thoughts and feelings of those praying the psalms are then shaped by the Word of God, rather than, as typical in private prayer, words originating out of individual thoughts, feelings, and desires.[22] In this way, borrowing an interpretive approach of Karl Barth, instead of focusing one's attention on interpreting Scripture, those praying the Psalms allow Scripture to interpret them, to challenge them to conform their ways to the way of God.[23] Furthermore, since the texts to be prayed corporately are chosen by the Church according to the liturgical season it is more likely that those praying the psalms will pray those psalms they may not feel like praying than if they chose the psalms to pray. In this manner those praying the psalms corporately in the context of the liturgy are formed in a more wholistic manner than if they only chose scriptural passages they feel drawn to.

The various types of psalms the Church chooses for her people to pray in the liturgy all are means by which those praying encounter words that form their thoughts, feelings, and desires. Psalms of lament educate one to complain properly by situating the complaint in the context of faith. As explained by Alobaidi, the typical divinely revealed pattern that psalms of

---

[22] Pope Benedict XVI, *Jesus of Nazareth, From the Baptism in the Jordan to the Transfiguration*, Kindle location 1998 of 5265.

[23] Donald Wood, *Barth's Theology of Interpretation* (Burlington: Ashgate Publishing Company, 2007), 172. Wood cites KD I/2, p. 829 (ET 737-8). "If the church is the assembly of those who hear the Word of God, in the last resort this necessarily means (for what would the hearing amount to otherwise?) the assembly of those who make use of it. But this, too, can mean only the assembly of those who are ready and willing that the Word of God on its part should make use of them... [I]nstead of our making use of scripture at every stage, it is scripture itself which uses us – the *uses scripturae* in which *scriptura* is not object but subject, and the hearer and reader is not subject but object."

lament follow is invoking God's presence, presenting to God the lament, requesting God for help, remembering salvation history in hope, and finally ending on a note of praise (Psalms 44, 60, 79, 80, 83, 85, 90).[24] A reason for this pattern, writes Miller, is therapeutic. Quoting Walter Brueggemann, Miller writes, "'There is a close correspondence between the anatomy of the lament psalm and the anatomy of the soul.' ... The lament actively embraces angst, grief, and anger, and then moves on to trust and thanksgiving. It's ancient Israelite therapy, so to speak."[25]

When it is remembered that the psalms were originally composed to be sung and often in a liturgical setting, then the psalms of lament reveal a level of comfort the Israelites had in expressing pain publicly. This freedom to publicly express sorrow, Miller opines, is less noticeable in the

---

[24] Alobaidi, class notes and lectures.

[25] Miller, *Understanding the Old Testament*, 323.

[26] Pete unseth [CC0], "Scroll of the Psalms," https://commons.wikimedia.org/wiki/File:Psalms_scroll.PNG.

liturgical songs of modern day Western Catholic liturgies.[27]

Another notable feature of the psalms of lament is that they at times, observes Miller, express anger at God, in particular Psalms 35 and 109. Psalm 35 intensely asks God, "How long, O Lord, will you look on? … You have seen, O Lord; be not silent! (Psalm 35:17, 22 *RSVCE*)." Similarly, Psalm 109 cries out, "Be not silent, O God of my praise! … He loved to curse; let curses come on him (Psalm 109:1, 17 *RSVCE*)." According to Miller, these statements of accusation directed to God are unique to Israel amidst ancient West Asian culture: "There's nothing comparable in the hymns of other ancient Near Eastern peoples. You get the impression that the ancient Egyptian god Amon-Ra would've struck you dead for speaking like this. Israelites believed God wants to hear what you're thinking, even if you're furious with him."[28]

The Israelites were also comfortable with singing psalms of lament directed against enemies. In identifying enemies as the source of lament, Psalm 60, as with other psalms, cries out, "O grant us help against the foe (Psalm 60:11 *RSVCE*)." The ease in which the psalms express "raw emotions," asserts Miller, including emotions with negative connotations of sorrow and anger, indicates that the Israelites who were inspired to compose and sing these psalms, "were convinced that God wanted to hear all of those emotions" including those directed against enemies.[29]

The enemies may be interpreted as, explains Alobaidi, "our disordered tendencies" but, he adds, it is important to also acknowledge that the enemies in the psalms often referred to concrete enemies of Israel or of the psalmist.[30] When applying the psalms to our lives, we also ought not to over spiritualize them but are to bring into our consciences those individuals who have hurt us so that, through the praying of the psalm, we

---

[27] Miller, *Understanding the Old Testament*, 319.
[28] Miller, *Understanding the Old Testament*, 320.
[29] Miller, *Understanding the Old Testament*, 323.
[30] Alobaidi, class notes and lectures.

acknowledge our angry feelings, thoughts, and desires and then allow them to be resolved in Jesus who forgave his enemies on the cross (Luke 23:34) and encourages us to do so in the Our Father prayer, "Forgive us our trespasses as we forgive those who have trespassed against us."

The awareness of enemies often is followed by the hope for a deliverer, a saving king. Psalms on kingship identified as "Royal Psalms" by Hermann Gunkel include Psalms 2, 18, 20, 21, 45, 72, 101, 110, 132, 144.[31] In reference to a saving king, Psalm 72 states, "Give the king your justice, O God. ... May he defend the cause of the poor of the people, give deliverance to the needy, and crush the oppressor. ... May all kings fall down before him, all nations serve him! (Psalm 72:1, 2, 11 *RSVCE*)." In commenting on passages which promise a future king, Benedict XVI argues that from a salvation historical perspective:

> it comes apparent that the promise of dominion over the nations-a promise taken over from the great kings of the East-is out of all proportion to the actual reality of the king on Mount Zion. He is only an insignificant ruler with a fragile power who ends up in exile, and afterward can be restored only for a brief time in dependence on the superpowers of the day. In other words, the royal oracle of Zion from the very beginning had to become a word of hope in a future king.[32]

Only on the cross did Jesus fully reveal himself as this promised king, as the title on the cross indicated. As Benedict XVI writes:

> [T]he title Messiah, "King of the Jews," is placed over the Cross –

---

[31] Hermann Gunkel, *An Introduction to the Psalms*, trans. James D. Nogalski (Macon, Mercer University Press, 1998), 99.

[32] Pope Benedict XVI, *Jesus of Nazareth, From the Baptism in the Jordan to the Transfiguration*, trans. Adrian J. Walker (New York: Double Day, 2007), Kindle location 4682 of 5265.

publicly displayed before the whole world. And it is permissible to place it there – in the three languages of the world of that time (cf. Jn 19:19f.) – because now there is no longer any chance of its being misunderstood. The Cross is his throne, and as such it gives the correct interpretation of this title.[33]

Psalms of lament, praise, thanks, confidence, wisdom, or other type may all be understood as pointing to the royal psalms in which under a future king, revealed in Christianity as Jesus, life with all its variety of expressions and emotional content is given its ultimate, definitive meaning.

Section Questions

1. How does corporate praying the psalms help to a balance prayer life and even emotional life that is informed by Revelation in its entirety? Include in your response: Psalms Interpreting the Reader vs. Reader Interpreting the Psalms.

2. Explain the divinely revealed therapeutic pattern of many lament psalms: Invocation, Presenting, Requesting, Recalling, Praising.

3. How do the Psalms approach raw emotions, including intense sorrow and anger? Include in your answer the following: Acknowledgement, God, Healing.

---

[33] Pope Benedict XVI, *Jesus of Nazareth, From the Baptism in the Jordan to the Transfiguration*, Kindle location 4478 of 5265.

4. How, according to Benedict XVI, is the promise of a future Zion King only fulfilled in Jesus?

Proverbs

Introduction

The book of Proverbs may be divided into Proverbs of Solomon (1:1-9:18; 10:1-22:16; 25:1-29:27) Wise Sayings (22:17-24:22; 24:23-34), Sayings

---

[1] Gustave Doré [Public domain], "Solomon writing Proverbs," https://commons.wikimedia.org/wiki/File:Dore_Solomon_Proverbs.png.

45

of Agur (30:1-14), Sayings of Lemuel's Mother (31:1-9), and Praise of a Good Wife (31:10-31). The many types of pithy wisdom sayings contained in these various collections are representative of a type of wisdom that is practical. As defined by Thomas Aquinas, this practical wisdom is "right reason applied to action" also known as prudence.[2]

Unlike the universal moral laws of the Ten Commandments that apply without exception, the prudential sayings of Proverbs, explains Hahn, "are concerned with choices to be made in particular circumstances" which may not be applicable in all circumstances.[3] Growing in wisdom, therefore, is ordinarily gained by experiencing life, learning from life, and learning from other's experiences. Then, this collected wisdom helps one to discern what choice is most suitable for a particular occasion. In describing this practical type of wisdom (*hokhma*, חָכְמָה), Miller compares it to learning how to sail:

> If you think about a sailboat, this is a good way to imagine *hokhma*. Learning to sail doesn't come from a set of rules. It's not something you can learn from books. You wouldn't study sailing only from books and then try to take a sailboat out on the Chesapeake Bay by yourself. It requires an apprenticeship; a learned ability that can't be reduced to rules on a page.[4]

However, clarifies Hahn, this does not mean that the prudential wisdom present in the Proverbs is completely relative. Instead, it provides expressions of basic "patterns and tendencies in life" observed by those

---

[2] Thomas Aquinas, "Question 47. Prudence, considered in itself, art. 2," newadvent.org, http://www.newadvent.org/summa/3047.htm.

[3] Scott Hahn, and Curtis Mitch, *Ignatius Catholic Study Bible, Proverbs, Ecclesiastes, and Song of Solomon Commentary, Notes, & Study Question*, (San Francisco: Ignatius Press, 2012), Loc. 291 of 6468.

[4] Robert D. Miller II, *Understanding the Old Testament* (Chantilly: The Teaching Company, 2019), 328.

who have experienced life and reflected on their experiences.[5]

Some of the identification of these patterns were borrowed by the Wisdom Literature from non-Jewish cultures, in particular the Egyptian *Instruction of Amenemope.*[6] This borrowing reflects the practical nature of wisdom since to grow in wisdom is to be open to learning from the experience of others, including outside of one's culture. Non-Israelite cultures (Mesopotamian, Arabian, Egyptian, and Greek) acquired a "practical skill" that, writes, Miller, "does not require a specific revelation from God."[7] According to Alobaidi, what distinguishes these possibly borrowed Egyptian wisdom sayings is the context of Proverbs. The ultimate context of Proverbs is salvation history leading up to fulfillment in Jesus Christ, the epitome in person of wisdom for all people, Jew and Gentile.[8]

In the following section, we will reflect on how fear of God and women

---

[5] Hahn and Mitch, *Ignatius Catholic Study Bible*, Loc. 302 of 6468.

[6] Hahn and Mitch, *Ignatius Catholic Study Bible*, Loc. 2832. According to Miller: "[T]he words of Lemuel, maybe Agur; 27:17 to 23:11 is practically a copy of an 11th-century BCE Egyptian text called the Instruction of Amenemope, with its own collection of maxims setting forth practical instructions for living. Eleven of the 30 sayings here are verbatim—the same. In fact, although 22:20 says, 'I have written thirty sayings,' there aren't actually 30 sayings in the book of Proverbs, but there are in Amenemope. If you look up the Wikipedia article on *Instruction of Amenemope*, you can see the quotations from Instruction and Proverbs laid out in matching pairs.

But there are several other Egyptian elements in Proverbs. So, 22:2 says, 'The Lord weighs the heart,' and it's again in 24:12. 'Weighing the heart' is actually an Egyptian image. In the judgment scene, after you die, your heart was placed on one side of a balance scale, and on the other side was put wisdom or Maat, which can be depicted as a feather but is also goddess. This 'weighing' is a way of judging you. And so, that image of weighing the heart, that's not a metaphor you would come up with independently. They borrowed this from Egypt." Miller, *Understanding the Old Testament*, 331.

[7] Miller, *Understanding the Old Testament*, 329.

[8] Joseph Alobaidi, class notes and lectures on *Wisdom Literature* (Washington, D.C.: Dominican House of Studies, Spring Semester 2008).

relate to wisdom.

9

Section Questions

1. Define wisdom as presented in Wisdom Literature by including the following terms: Prudence, Experience, Relativity, Patterns, Tendencies, Unique Context.

---

[9] Artist is Robert Lewis Reid (1862–1929). Photographed 2007 by Carol Highsmith (1946–), who explicitly placed the photograph in the public domain. [Public domain], "Understanding, mural by Robert Lewis Reid. Second Floor, North Corridor. Library of Congress Thomas Jefferson Building, Washington, D.C. Caption underneath reads: WISDOM IS THE PRINCIPAL THING THEREFORE GET WISDOM AND WITH ALL THY GETTING GET VNDERSTANDING," https://commons.wikimedia.org/wiki/File:Understanding -Reid-Highsmith.jpeg.

Fear of God and Lady Wisdom

Although fear is an emotion, this is not what is most essential to the definition of fear in Proverbs. As Benedict XVI clarifies, "In biblical language…this 'fear' is not fright. It is recognition of the mystery of divine transcendence."[10] The proper attitude towards Almighty God is awe, is fear. Since God is omni-present, we are to "continue in the fear of the Lord all the day (23:17 *RSVCE*)." Practically, this means that, argues Alobaidi, fear of God is essentially defined by the degree a person is disposed to obey God who is to be obeyed since He is absolutely holy.[11]

The Ten Commandments are the standard that determines obedience to God. They are the structure in which we are to live as children of one common Heavenly Father. The structure provided by the Ten Commandments is the home in which we are free to be ourselves in a fulfilling way, as social, relational creatures who give way to our brothers if justice and charity, determined by the Ten Commandments, indicate that a desire that we may to act upon would rupture family harmony.

The temptation to run away from home, run away from the structure provided by the Ten Commandments is motivated by the desire to experience another type of freedom, a freedom that is only determined by the degree of power an individual has to act upon any desire they feel. Since this autonomous freedom is contrary to our created social natures, experiences of this type of individualistic freedom will never be satisfying and always will be disappointing despite brief moments of exciting elation that quickly vanish, since the joy is false, ephemeral joy that unlike true joy is not lasting and enduring. True joy is lasting since it is rooted in stable relationships that uphold it, principally the relationship with God.

Proverbs warns us from wanting to experience the false kind of

---

[10] Benedict XVI, *Day by Day with Pope Benedict XVI*, ed. Peter John Cameron (San Francisco: Ignatius Press, 2006), 278.

[11] Alobaidi, class notes and lectures.

freedom that is outside of our family home created for us by God that only can be lived in if we follow the Ten Commandments: "Let not your heart envy sinners, but continue in the fear of the Lord all the day (Proverbs 23:17 *RSVCE*)." In its biblical context, sinners, defines Pitre, are people who are breaking the Ten Commandments, the Torah, in a grave, public way.[12] The freedom these people live is autonomous freedom, freedom outside of the home provided by the Ten Commandments. Like the Prodigal Son in the gospel parable, they experience fleeting types of happiness but which never satisfies and always leaves them, at some level, longing to go back home, where they will experience, what Benedict XVI, calls, "shared freedom."[13] The autonomous freedom of sinners, he explains, that is lawless, where might makes right, destroys the partici-pated reality of social freedom.[14] May we heed Proverbs 23 and not envy this freedom but rather in fear, in awe of God, recognize it as false freedom, freedom that can never bring true, lasting happiness.

Fear of God that maintains us in true freedom, Alobaidi comments, involves experiencing contrary feelings at the same time, the feeling of "being attracted and [the] feeling of being distant."[15] The feeling of attraction is due to being created by God and for God in whom alone do we find deep, perfect rest. The feeling of being distant from God and even a fear of coming near to God, whom we also at the same time feel drawn to, is in turn due to an awareness of our lack of perfection, of our need for purification from sin.[16]

In describing fear of God in respect to sin, proverbs 8 states, "the fear of the Lord is hatred of evil (8:13 *RSVCE*)." Since all fallen human beings

---

[12] Brant Pitre, "The Twenty-fourth Sunday of Ordinary Time, (Year C)," catholicproductions.com, 3.

[13] Benedict XVI Joseph Ratzinger, *Faith and Politics Selected Writings*, trans. Michael J. Miller (San Francisco: Ignatius Press, 2018), Kindle Location, 2121.

[14] Benedict XVI, *Faith and Politics Selected Writings*, Kindle Location, 2121.

[15] Alobaidi, class notes and lectures.

[16] Alobaidi, class notes and lectures.

are impure before God who alone is all holy, and since all are created by God for God, both parts of the following proverb apply to all human beings, "He who walks in uprightness fears the Lord, but he who is devious in his ways despises him (Proverbs 14:2 *RSVCE*)."

These two contrary emotions within the fear of Lord Alobaidi explains in reference to the times before the Fall of Adam and Eve and after their Fall. Before the first sin of human beings, Adam and Eve experienced Paradise where the only type of fear they felt was that of the fear of a loving children who fear doing anything that would damage their love relationship with God the Father. After the Fall, though, their understanding of God became distorted by their sinful state and they now feared God like one fears a vindictive master who will quickly accuse, judge, and severely punish those who disobey him.

---

[17] "Early Christian depiction of Adam and Eve in the Catacombs of Marcellinus and Peter." https://commons.wikimedia.org/wiki/File:Adam_%26_Eve_02.jpg.

In addition, unlike the time before the Fall when Adam and Eve were totally occupied with gazing upon the Lord, through creation, and through each other, after the Fall, they turned their gaze in servile fear on themselves, with heads down in shame. This gaze, comments Alobaidi made them intensely aware of their nakedness and associated weakness that before the Fall did not bother them. Prior to the Fall, their naked weakness, their state of being relatively weaponless, defenseless creatures was not a concern for Adam and Eve since they were taken up with loving God and relied on the strength that God gave them.

This relationship of love was shattered by Adam and Eve's choosing to sin. Afterwards, they hid in excessive, servile fear from the Divine Father whom they once loved with all their heart, mind, body and soul. Not only was their understanding of God distorted by sin but also their relationship to one another was wounded. No longer did Adam and Eve see each other as companions, explains Alobaidi, but instead viewed one another as competitors in an adversarial relationship of who could dominate the other, whether by force or emotional manipulation.[18]

The coming of the New Testament in the person of Jesus Christ did not bring to a complete end the fallen world characterized by excessive fear that Adam and Eve even felt towards one another. Rather, the New Testament times, which we currently are in, is, writes Benedict XVI, a "in-between" state, where we experience the Kingdom of Heaven in a here but not yet perfect, definitive state. For this reason, states Benedict XVI:

> The Testaments should not be understood as a simple succession, a merely temporal juxtaposition and sequence, so that with the beginning of the New the Old would have only the value of a historical reminiscence. Rather, there is a genuine interpenetration, so that the Old Testament continues to live in the New Testament, and the latter

---

[18] Alobaidi, class notes and lectures.

is and can be only in this mutual dependence; the definitive abolition of the Old and its elevation into the merely New belong to the world to come, not to our "in-between" state.[19]

He then applies this Catholic understanding of the relationship of the Old Testament to the New Testament to "the relation between fear of the Lord and love of God"[20]:

The New Testament does not simply abolish fear absolutely. But neither is it true that fear remains there as a separate act alongside of love, in such a way that their mutual proportions are shifted: for instance, fear is minimized, and love maximized. It is not a simple juxtaposition. Rather, the act of fear remains as such in the love and gives it its special meaning; more precisely: the act of love enters into the previous propaedeutic act of fear and transforms it without canceling it out; rather, it really retains it within itself as the "matter" that makes it possible.[21]

The perfect transformation of fear by love where there is no longer any imperfect fear that a slave has towards a master but rather only fear a loving son has towards his father only occurs after death when, God willing, we fully enter into heaven, in a definitive relationship with Jesus, head and members, including the saints in heaven. In describing this perfect state of love that fully transforms fear Saint Hilary writes:

For us the fear of God consists wholly in love, and perfect love of God brings out fear of him to its perfection. Our love for God is entrusted

---

[19] Benedict XVI, *Dogma and Preaching: Applying Christian Doctrine to Daily Life*, trans. Michael J. Miller (San Francisco: Ignatius Press, 2011), 252.

[20] Benedict XVI, *Dogma and Preaching*, 252-253.

[21] Benedict XVI, *Dogma and Preaching*, 252-253.

with its own responsibility: to observe his counsels, to obey his laws, to trust his promises. Let us hear what Scripture says: *And now, Israel, what does the Lord your God ask of you except to fear the Lord your God and walk in all his ways and love him and keep his commandments with your whole heart and your whole soul, so that it may be well for you?*[22]

Similarly, Venerable Bede distinguishes imperfect fear from perfect that is completely transformed by heavenly love with:

"The fear of the Lord is the beginning of knowledge." Two things constitute the fear of the Lord: first, the servanthood which is called the beginning of knowledge or wisdom and, second, the friendship which accompanies the perfection of wisdom. Servile fear is the beginning of wisdom because whoever begins to taste it after the error of sins is corrected by this first divine fear, lest he be led into torments. But perfect love casts this fear out. Holy fear of the Lord then follows, remaining forever, and is augmented by charity, not removed by it. This is the fear with which the good son is afraid, lest he offend the eyes of his most loving father in the least degree. For the soul is still afraid with elementary servile fear, lest it suffer punishment from an angry Lord. But each fear will come to an end in the future life. Charity, however, never passes away, but will remain perpetually in the fulness of wisdom, which is to know the one, true God and Jesus Christ whom he has sent.[23]

---

[22] *The Liturgy of the Hours*, II (New York: Catholic Book Publishing Co., 1976), "From a treatise on the psalms by Saint Hilary, bishop (Ps. 127, 1-3: CSEL 24, 628-630)," 187.

[23] J. Robert Wright (ed.), *Ancient Christian Commentary on Scripture, Old Testament IX, Proverbs, Ecclesiastes, Song of Solomon,* "Commentary on Proverbs, 1.1.7.," (Downers Grove: IVP Academic, 2005), 27.

The first chapter of Proverbs can be interpreted as a reference to Eve's state prior to the Fall when her fear was perfectly informed by charity. In personifying wisdom as an upright, loving woman Proverbs states, "Wisdom cries aloud in the street; in the markets she raises her voice; on the top of the walls she cries out; at the entrance of the city gates she speaks (Proverbs 1:20-21 *RSVCE*)." If listened to, Lady Wisdom promises, "You will be saved from the loose woman, from the adventuress with her smooth words ... for her house sinks down to death (Wisdom 2:16-18 *RSVCE*)." As the first chapter opens with a wise woman, the last chapter ends in praise of two women, the mother of Lemuel, king of Massa, and a good wife (Proverbs 31). King Lemuel's mother counsels the king to be sexually chaste, to drink alcohol with moderation, and to take care of the dying, the poor, the needy, and those who have no one to defend them (Proverbs 31:6-9 *RSVCE*)." The virtuous wife is similarly praised for her care for the poor and needy.

In contrast, Lady Folly is described as encouraging and enticing those she meets into promiscuity (Proverbs 7:5-23; 9:17). Like Lady Wisdom, Lady Folly, Miller comments, accompanies us in this life as our companion. Unlike Lady Wisdom who gently leads us down the path of virtue and deep joyful peace, Lady Folly attempts to seduce us down the path of sinful excitement that leaves one feeling empty and dissatisfied.[24] In describing these seductive ways, Hahn comments, "Seduction, especially sexual seduction, probes for weak points in a person's character, such as a need to be found attractive or a desire for power or adventure. What are some weak points where an effort to seduce might attract you? How should you protect yourself?"[25] The seduction that many Israelites faced at the time when Proverbs was being written was similar but different from the typical modern-day kinds of seduction. As Pitre points out, in the biblical times of Proverbs, the pagan liturgical cults promoted

---

[24] Miller, *Understanding the Old Testament*, 332.

[25] Hahn and Mitch, *Ignatius Catholic Study Bible*, loc. 3422-3423.

promiscuous fertility cults which offered followers communion with a divine being through sexual activity with a temple prostitute. The texts in Proverbs that contrast Lady Folly with Lady Wisdom indicate that the type of seduction associated with Lady Folly involved the pagan fertility cults. This is evident in that, writes Bergsma and Pitre:

> both Lady Wisdom and Lady Folly are characterized as calling out to men from "the heights" and "high places" of the city (cf. Prov 8:2 - 4, 9: 13-14). The heights of any ancient city, including Jerusalem, were the sacred precincts, where the temple or temples were located. Thus, Lady Wisdom and Lady Folly are portrayed as competing forms of worship. Lady Wisdom represents the cult of the Lord, characterized by marriage and covenant fidelity; whereas Lady Folly represents foreign cults, characterized by fertility rituals and promiscuity.[26]

Section Questions

1. Define Fear of God as presented in Wisdom Literature and as transformed by the New Testament. Include the following in your response: Fright, Awe, 10 Commandments, Envy of Sinners, Closeness, Distance, Filial Fear, Servile Fear.

2. Contrast Lady Wisdom with Lady Folly by including the following terms: Seduction to False Freedom, Persuasion to True Freedom, Pagan Fertility Cults.

---

[26] John Bergsma and Brant Pitre, *A Catholic Introduction to the Bible, Volume I* (San Francisco: Ignatius Press, 2018), Kindle location 13408.

Typology in Proverbs

27

Lady Wisdom is perfectly embodied in Jesus' mother, Mary. This is particularly evident in a popular title of Mary, Our Lady Seat of Wisdom. Wisdom is also understood as fulfilled in Christ the Word of the Father spoken in the love of the Holy Spirit. The Fathers of the Church interpreted Proverbs 8:22 as specifically referring to Christ, "The Lord created me at the beginning of his work the first of his acts of old

---

[27] Artist is Robert Lewis Reid (1862–1929). Photographed 2007 by Carol Highsmith (1946–), who explicitly placed the photograph in the public domain. [Public domain], "*Wisdom*, mural by Robert Lewis Reid. Second Floor, North Corridor. Library of Congress Thomas Jefferson Building, Washington, D.C. Caption underneath reads "KNOWLEDGE COMES BVT WISDOM LINGERS." https://commons.wikimedia.org/wiki/File:Wisdom-Reid-Highsmith.jpeg.

(*RSVCE*)." This typological manner of interpreting Proverbs 8:22 is first explicitly made in the New Testament.

In direct reference to Sirach 24:3 and Proverbs 8:22-31 St. Paul, observes Miller, writes: "He is the image of the invisible God, the first-born of all creation… He is before all things, and in him all things hold together (Colossians 1:15, 17 *RSVCE*)." In addition, John's Gospel similarly opens with, "In the beginning was the Word, and the Word was with God, and the Word was God. He was in the beginning with God; all things were made through him, and without him was not anything made that was made (John 1:1-3 *RSVCE*)." John and St. Paul's identification of primordial Wisdom with Jesus was providentially influenced by ancient Jewish tradition that primordial Wisdom, including Lady Wisdom, is Torah, is the Ten Commandments given to Moses on Mount Sinai. The biblical (by some understood as apocryphal) ancient Jewish book of Baruch (c. 200-100 B.C.) states: "Learn where is wisdom … This is the book of the commandments of God, and the law that endureth forever."[28] The law of Wisdom has existed forever and was presented to Moses at Sinai since as Sirach teaches, "I am forth from the mouth of the Most High, the first-born before all creatures (Sirach 24:3 *RSVCE*)."[29]

In continuity with the New Testament's recognition of Jesus as the fulfillment of Wisdom, Gregory of Nyssa comments on Proverbs 8:22: "The phrase 'created me' refers not to the divine and the uncompounded but, as has been said, to that which had been assumed, in accordance with the divine plan, from our created nature."[30] With this explanation, Gregory of Nyssa argues against the Arian Eunomius that the word create

---

[28] "The Book of Baruch with the Epistle of Jeremiah," biblestudyforlife.com, http://biblestudyforlife.com/PDF/Baruch.pdf, 3:14: 4:1.

[29] Miller, *Understanding the Old Testament*, 335.

[30] J. Robert Wright (ed.), *Ancient Christian Commentary on Scripture, Old Testament IX, Proverbs, Ecclesiastes, Song of Solomon*, "Gregory of Nyssa, Against Eunomius 3.1.50.," (IVP Academic: Downers Grove, 2005), 134.

may apply to Christ but only to Christ's human, created nature.

In support of the Church Fathers interpretation of Proverbs chapter eight that Christ fulfills the mediating role from the "the foundations of the earth" by being "beside" God (Proverbs 8:29-30 *RSVCE*)," Hahn appeals to 1 Corinthians 1:30 and John 1:2, Colossians 1:16, and Hebrews 1:2, which describes Christ in similar words as Proverbs describes Wisdom:

But of Him you are in Christ Jesus, who became for us wisdom from God—and righteousness and sanctification and redemption (1 Corinthians 1:30 *RSVCE*).

He was in the beginning with God (John 1:2 *RSVCE*).

...for in him all things were created, in heaven and on earth, visible and invisible, whether thrones or dominions or principalities or authorities—all things were created through him and for him (Colossians 1:16 *RSVCE*)."

... but in these last days he has spoken to us by a Son, whom he appointed the heir of all things, through whom also he created the world (Hebrews 1:2 *RSVCE*).

The Divine Father ceaselessly speaks the Word of his Son in the love of the Holy Spirit. God does so by his abiding presence that upholds all creation. The Word of God is, "living and active, sharper than any two-edged sword, piercing to the division of soul and spirit, of joints and marrow, and discerning the thoughts and intentions of the heart (Hebrews 4:12 *RSVCE*)." Similarly, states Jesus, the Holy Spirit also challenges us right to the depths of our beings as one who "will convince the world of sin and of righteousness and of judgment (John 16:8 *RSVCE*)." Proverbs also describes God as one who convicts even the one who deems himself "pure in his own eyes" for the "Lord weighs the spirit (Proverbs 16:2 *RSVCE*)." This conviction of sin differs from the accusing nature of the diabolic spirit who accuses to divide one definitively from God with no desire for there to be a reordering of the divided person back into right relationship with God.

May we remain open to the Holy Spirit who both consoles, convicts, and even through "the word of God" divides "soul and spirit ... joints and marrow (Hebrews 4:12 *RSVCE*) all, though, with the intention of reordering a person into right relationship with God and, through God, with their brothers and sisters. As a way to be sensitive to the Holy Spirit, to the Wisdom of God, Hahn encourages "to ask the Holy Spirit to purify [our motives] ... even to convict you of sin so you can repent where needed."[31] The more the Holy Spirit is heeded the more we will develop a sensitive conscience where even words of flattery which ordinarily do not prick people's consciences will move one to repentance for as Proverbs states, "It is not good to eat much honey, so be sparing of complimentary words (Proverbs 25:27 *RSVCE*)." Directing our attention to the *Catechism of the Catholic Church*, Hahn points out that the sin of flattery that Proverbs identifies can be a grave sin:

> Every word or attitude is forbidden which by *flattery, adulation, or complaisance* encourages and confirms another in malicious acts and perverse conduct. Adulation is a grave fault if it makes one an accomplice in another's vices or grave sins. Neither the desire to be of service nor friendship justifies duplicitous speech. Adulation is a venial sin when it only seeks to be agreeable, to avoid evil, to meet a need, or to obtain legitimate advantages.[32]

---

[31] Hahn and Mitch, *Ignatius Catholic Study Bible*, loc. 3557.

[32] "Catechism of the Catholic Church, no. 2480," vatican.va, http://www.vatican.va/archive/ccc_css/archive/catechism/p3s2c2a8.htm;   Scott

Encouraging greater sensitivity of conscience, Psalm Nineteen laments, "But who can discern his errors? Clear me from hidden faults. Keep back your servant also from presumptuous sins; let them not have dominion over me! (12-13)." In commenting on these verses, Benedict XVI writes, "No longer seeing one's guilt, the falling silent of conscience in so many areas, is an even more dangerous sickness of the soul than the guilt that one still recognizes as such. He who no longer notices that killing is a sin has fallen farther than the one who still recognizes the shamefulness of his actions."[33]

Section Questions

1. How does Jesus fulfill Proverbs 8:22 "The LORD created me at the beginning of his work, the first of his acts of old"? Include the following in your answer: Wisdom, Arianism, Gregory of Nyssa, Human Nature, Divine Nature.

Hahn, and Curtis Mitch, *Ignatius Catholic Study Bible, Proverbs, Ecclesiastes, and Song of Solomon Commentary, Notes, & Study Question*, (San Francisco: Ignatius Press, 2012), loc. 3736-3737.

[33] Benedict XVI Joseph Ratzinger, *Faith and Politics Selected Writings*, trans. Michael J. Miller (San Francisco: Ignatius Press, 2018), Kindle Location, 1220.

Ecclesiastes

Introduction

The Hebrew title for the Latin transliteration of the Greek title Ecclesiastes is *Qōheleth* (קֹהֶלֶת). *Qōheleth* is based on the word *qahal* (קָהָל), meaning "assembly, convocation, congregation."[2] Bergsma and Pitre liter-

---

[1] "*Vanitas* by Harmen Steenwijck," https://commons.wikimedia.org/wiki/File:Harmen_Steenwijck_-_Vanitas.JPG.

[2] "6951. qahal," biblehub.com, https://biblehub.com/hebrew/6951.htm.

ally translate *Qōheleth* as "one who calls an assembly."[3] The Greek title Ekklēsiastēs (Ἐκκλησιαστής) similarly means an assembly and congregation. The English word ecclesial originates from this Greek word.

Ecclesiastes comes after Proverbs and before the Song of Songs. Since the third century, according to Hahn, these three books have been understood by early Christian writers as representing stages of the spiritual life. According to one common traditional interpretation, Ecclesiastes represents the stage of fighting vices and growing in virtue, also known as the purgative stage. The second illuminative stage where one experiences integration, deeper peace, and spiritual enlightenment is represented by the insightful wisdom of the book of Proverbs. Finally, the love poetry of the Song of Songs represents the final stage in the spiritual journey, the unitive stage, when by passing through various nights of the soul (sensual and spiritual as John of the Cross explains) the person becomes ever more united to Jesus Christ.[4]

Although it is clear that Ecclesiastes focuses on vices (self-indulgence, vanity, disordered desires, folly) and virtues (order, friendship, wisdom, reverence, humility, obedience), it is difficult to quickly identify a clear structure within Ecclesiastes. However, a structure is identifiable. As presented by Bergsma and Pitre, the structure is as follows: prologue (1:1 -11) on vanity, first part on vanity (1:12 - 18; 2:1 - 6:9), second part on vanity (2:1 - 6:9), third part on ignorance (6:10 - 11:6), fourth part on age (11:7 – 12), conclusion with an epilogue (12:9-14).[5] Another way to approach Ecclesiastes in a systematic manner is by themes.

---

[3] John Bergsma and Brant Pitre, *A Catholic Introduction to the Bible, Volume I* (San Francisco: Ignatius Press, 2018), Kindle location 13622.

[4] Scott Hahn, and Curtis Mitch, *Ignatius Catholic Study Bible, Proverbs, Ecclesiastes, and Song of Solomon Commentary, Notes, & Study Question*, (San Francisco: Ignatius Press, 2012), loc. 3944-3948; Bergsma and Pitre, *A Catholic Introduction to the Bible*, Kindle location 13638.

[5] Bergsma and Pitre, *A Catholic Introduction to the Bible*, Kindle location 13650.

Section Questions

1. What is the meaning of the Hebrew title *Qōheleth* and the Greek title *Ekklēsiastēs?*

2. According to tradition, how do the following correspond to one another and why? Purgative, Unitive, Illuminative | Song of Songs, Proverbs, Ecclesiastes.

Themes

Alobaidi identifies the main themes in Ecclesiastes as: newness, meaning, vanity, pessimism (death), God's providential design, and fear of God.[6]

The first chapter opens with Qoheleth asserting, "All is vanity." This is followed by numerous examples of the cyclical nature of time including the repeated cyclic nature of one generation to the next, the predictable cycles of the sun, the ever-blowing nature of wind, and the constant flow of streams. All of these examples, argues Qoheleth, demonstrate that there "is nothing new under the sun (Ecclesiastes 1:9 *RSVCE*)," only appearances of newness.

Since, continues Qoheleth, everything "is vanity and a striving after wind (Ecclesiastes 1:14 *RSVCE*)," even the search for meaning, wisdom, and knowledge is also "but a striving after wind (Ecclesiastes 1:17 *RSVCE*)." All, no matter their mastery of wisdom and knowledge, will meet the same end, and wise or fool after passing from this world will eventually in time be "long forgotten (Ecclesiastes 2:16 *RSVCE*)." This

---

[6] Joseph Alobaidi, class notes and lectures on *Wisdom Literature* (Washington, D.C.: Dominican House of Studies, Spring Semester 2008).

pessimistic view of life is evident right in the word "vanity" that is repeated throughout Ecclesiastes.

The Hebrew word that English bibles translate as vanity is *hebel* (הֶבֶל). *Hebel* literally means "vapor, breath."[8] Hahn observes that the Hebrew word for Cain's brother Abel, whom Cain killed, is also *Hebel*. Abel's name is fitting for him since his life was like a breath that is here and then quickly vanishes.[9] Nothing that Abel did, even his regular worship of God, saved him from fratricide. This lesson on the vanity of life, which Ecclesiastes repeatedly emphasizes, comments Alobaidi, the prophetic dimension of

---

[7] William-Adolphe Bouguereau [Public domain], "*The First Mourning* (Adam and Eve mourn the death of Abel); oil on canvas 1888 painting by William-Adolphe Bouguereau," https://commons.wikimedia.org/wiki/File: Bouguereau-The_First_Mourning-1888.jpg.

[8] "Strong's Concordance, 1892. hebel," biblehub.com, https://biblehub.com/hebrew/1892.htm.

[9] Hahn and Mitch, *Ignatius Catholic Study Bible*, loc. 3843-3847.

the book, for:

> The prophet's function is to remind you that your effort is useless: your armies, wealth, etc. If you continue to believe in the efficiency of your means to attain salvation you will be destroyed. The prophet wants to bring you to zero hope about your own means of salvation, then God will come and help you. The prophet reminds us to acknowledge that by yourself you will liberate by producing victims. If you continue to be the author of your own salvation you will fail and produce victims even though your intention was to be a redeemer. When you have zero hope in your effort without the help of God your heart will become clean and pure. ... The prophets came in order to have God as the source of your salvation and not to have other sources: state, military power, self, wealth, individual, natural gifts, doctors, technology, science ... When God knows that you have no hope other than God then he will come. Qoheleth tries to humble the reader so that he will trust and hope more in God.[10]

As the reader trusts more in God and prioritizes all around God as the ultimate end of life, then the teaching of Ecclesiastes is clearly understood as leading one to hope and not to despair, hope in God as our savior. In support of this positive interpretation of Ecclesiastes as fully situated in Wisdom Literature, Miller comments:

> Ecclesiastes is read on one of the most important holidays in the Jewish calendar. And not read on some depressing holiday: it is read on the Feast of Sukkot or Booths, which is the most joyous of all Jewish holidays. And the blessing that is recited before it states: "Rejoice in your festival and be altogether joyous on this day of celebration we

---

[10] Alobaidi, class notes and lectures.

rejoice in. On this day, a book of wisdom is set before us. On this day, we enjoy the gifts of rich harvest goodness. On this day, we ponder teachings with which we can dower all our days with joy.[11]

As joyful Wisdom Literature, Ecclesiastes introduces one to God's view of reality, which includes God's providential design where "[f]or everything there is a season, and time for every matter under heaven … a time to plant, and a time to pluck up what is planted (Ecclesiastes 3:1 *RSVCE*)." With these words, Sister Joan Chittister comments, God teaches us to be patient and accepting of our role in time and not to enviously want to be someone whom we are not, or to act in a way that is the future mission of someone else. Many of us are simply called by God to sow, to plant seeds of God's goodness and grace, and then, after we die, others are called by God to reap the crop of what has been sown. The sower should not grow impatient, and the reaper should not become proud by attributing all the work to himself, since he was merely the reaper of others' labor.[12]

Another way of interpreting the opening verses of chapter three is by understanding them not from the perspectives of multiple life spans but from the perspective of one life which God wants to be balanced by a variety of human experiences: joy, sorrow, seeking, losing, talking, being silent, loving, hating, etc. Being properly balanced necessarily means not falling into idolatry. When a created good is made into an idol, it is fixated upon excessively. The cure is loving God above all created reality. Then, our love of God relativizes all other loves causing us to live with healthy detachment from created reality in a way that we can embrace the created good, can rejoice in the created good but without making any created good

---

[11] Robert D. Miller II, *Understanding the Old Testament* (Chantilly: The Teaching Company, 2019), 364.

[12] Joan Chittister, *For Everything a Season* (New York: Orbis Book, 2013), 62-63.

a god. "When we distort a good," comments Chittister, we "wrench it, inflate it, become consumed by it and no other, we ourselves turn good into evil. That's why there is, certainly, 'a time to refrain from embracing.'"[13] Without balancing embracing with refraining from embracing, the desire for created good can increase, writes Chittister, "More, more, more. Until dissipated, crazed, bored, restless, [we] come to realize that too much of a good thing is as denigrating of the human soul as deprivation itself. [We] come to understand that what [we] lacked in life—the ability to refrain from embracing—is what [we] needed most in life."[14]

If an idolized created good that a person refuses to stop embracing dies, is lost, or is removed from the person, then the natural result is intense sorrow that is not balanced by joy, and ultimately by love of God. As Chittister observes, "Whatever we are not prepared to lose we are enslaved to maintain—at any cost."[15] And when we lose what we are enslaved to, we can easily fall into despair. Ecclesiastes' "spirituality of balance"[16] encourages a self-examination on what causes us sorrow, for, Chittister adds, "where sorrow resides lies the clue to what we really love in life."[17] Accusing herself before anyone else, Chittister asks, "I must demand of myself to know why I stay at what is not good for me, why I continue to do what I do not want to do, why I wear myself out straining for one thing at the expense of another that is equally good, equally important to the human condition."[18] Ecclesiastes' promotion of balance in life, of rejoicing but not excessively, and crying, but not to despair, is ultimately regulated by God as the Lord of History.

---

[13] Chittister, *For Everything a Season*, 118.
[14] Chittister, *For Everything a Season*, 119.
[15] Chittister, *For Everything a Season*, 22.
[16] Chittister, *For Everything a Season*, 122.
[17] Chittister, *For Everything a Season*, 110.
[18] Chittister, *For Everything a Season*, 122.

The more it is acknowledged that God is the Lord of history who subtly orders and balances our experiences in life, the more readily it is understood that "He has made everything beautiful in time; also he has put eternity into man's mind (Ecclesiastes 3:11 *RSVCE*)." The eternity of God that human beings have been created with is a participation in God's timeless, eternal now dimension that transcends space and time while at the same time upholding and interfacing with space and time. A way to be aware of this heavenly, eternal dimension in the world is, recommends Ecclesiastes, to live in the present moment without excessive concern for the past or future: "So I saw that there is nothing better than that a man should enjoy his work, for that is his lot (Ecclesiastes 3:22 *RSVCE*)." Similarly, Ecclesiastes teaches, "Go, eat your bread with enjoyment, and drink your wine with a merry heart; for God has already approved what you do (Ecclesiastes 9:7 *RSVCE*)." This God centered approach to enjoying life is essentially different, asserts Miller, from a hedonism:

> In no case is it "eat and drink for tomorrow we die." The pursuit of pleasure was dismissed as empty very early on in the book. Sensual pleasures are by no stretch of the imagination put forward as an end and aim in life. But that's the point: the power to enjoy life is itself a divine gift, and it mocks those who furtively grasp for pleasure on their own. … It matters how you employ the gift, beneficially or shamefully, more than your wisdom or your knowledge matter. Life is a gift from God, and you have to accept it as a gift not with anxiety but with joy. And failure to enjoy life's blessings is a sin.[19]

Enjoyment of the present moment is safeguarded by fear of God, essentially consisting of keeping God's commandments, "for this is the whole duty of man (Ecclesiastes 12:13 *RSVCE*)." In fulfilling his duty, man

---

[19] Miller, *Understanding the Old Testament*, 366-367.

experiences peace and joy as he acts in accordance with how he has been created. The fear of God referred to in the epilogue, reminds Alobaidi, "is not about fear of being punished; it is about losing love."[20] The love referred to is the love of God since only God is eternal without any conditions and therefore only God is the stable reality of all reality. As Alobaidi asserts, the only reality that Ecclesiastes does not identify as vain is God, for compared with God all other reality is like a breath, is insubstantial, and only has meaning when directed towards God; otherwise, it ends in vanity, in meaninglessness.[21]

Section Questions

1. What is the literal and typical Scriptural translation of Abel's name (*Hebel* הֶבֶל), and how is the meaning of Abel's name related to Abel's murder by Cain?

2. How, according to Ecclesiastes are all things vain? Include in the your answer the following: God, Creation, Spirituality of Balance, Hedonism and Enjoyment of Created Reality, Reality that is not Vain.

---

[20] Alobaidi, class notes and lectures.
[21] Alobaidi, class notes and lectures.

Song of Solomon

Introduction

The Song of Solomon, also known as the Song of Songs or Canticles are love poems between a man and a woman. They are attributed to, and possibly in part written by, King Solomon. In Jewish tradition, according

---

[1] Egon Tschirch [CC BY-SA 3.0 de (https://creativecommons.org/licenses/by-sa/3.0/de/deed.en)], *"Study G,"* https://commons.wikimedia.org/wiki/File:Egon_Tschirch-_Hohelied_Studie_G_(high_resolution).jpg.

to Hahn, the Song of Songs was written by Solomon in his youth when his passion for women and love of the sensual world were intense. As he aged, as he mellowed and his strong emotions waned, Solomon grew in prudence and composed Proverbs. Finally, in his old age, while reflecting back upon his youth and middle age, he wrote Ecclesiastes where he acknowledges the vanity of many of his pursuits he once considered as very important and even essential to life.[2]

The first of these three books, the Song of Solomon, can be interpreted in a variety of ways that are intended by God to be complementary. These include an erotic love interpretation, a divine love interpretation, and a liturgical interpretation. The latter two interpretations can also be subdivided. The divine love interpretation may refer to God's love for Israel, God's love for the Church, and God's love for an individual person. The liturgical interpretation may refer to Israelite liturgical worship or to Christian liturgical worship.

Section Questions

1. Traditionally how do the following correspond to Solomon when young, middle aged, and old, and why? Ecclesiastes, Proverbs, Song of Songs

2. How do the following interpretations of the Song of Solomon differ from one another: Erotic, Divine, and Liturgical?

---

[2] Scott Hahn, and Curtis Mitch, *Ignatius Catholic Study Bible, Proverbs, Ecclesiastes, and Song of Solomon Commentary, Notes, & Study Question*, (San Francisco: Ignatius Press, 2012), loc. 5865-5887.

Human Love Interpretation

In referring to the human love that is depicted in the Song of Solomon, John Paul II writes:

> The truth of love, which is proclaimed by the Song of Songs, cannot be separated from the "language of the body." The truth of love, in fact, *enables the same* "language of the body" to be reread in the truth. This is also the truth of the increasing closeness of the spouses, which grows through love: and closeness means also initiation into the mystery of the person, without, however, implying its violation. ... The truth of the increasing closeness of the spouses through love develops in the subjective dimension "of the heart," of affection and sentiment, and this truth allows one to discover the other in oneself as a gift and, in some sense, to "tasting him" within oneself. [3]

With these words, John Paul II affirms the goodness of the sensual nature of human love. This is particularly evident in describing spouses "tasting" the spouse within themselves. Similarly, Benedict XVI also affirms the goodness of erotic love by insisting that erotic, receiving love and agape, giving love:

> can never be completely separated. The more the two, in their different aspects, find a proper unity in the one reality of love, the more the true nature of love in general is realized. Even if *eros* at first mainly covetous and ascending, a fascination for the great promise of happiness, in drawing near to the other, it is less and less concerned with itself, increasingly seeks the happiness of the other, is concerned

---

[3] John Paul II, *Man and Woman He Created Them, A Theology of the Body*, trans. Michael Waldstein (Pauline Books & Media: Boston, 2006), Kindle Location 11821. The following was cited, General Audience of June 6, 1984.

more and more with the beloved, bestows itself and wants to "be there
for" the other. The element of *agape* thus enters into this love, for
otherwise *eros* is impoverished and even loses its own nature. On the
other hand, man cannot live by oblative, descending love alone. He
cannot always give, he must also receive. Anyone who wishes to give
love must also receive love as a gift. Certainly, as the Lord tells us, one
can become a source from which rivers of living water flow
(cf. *Jn* 7:37-38). Yet to become such a source, one must constantly
drink anew from the original source, which is Jesus Christ, from
whose pierced heart flows the love of God (cf. *Jn* 19:34).[4]

The Song of Solomon can be interpreted as referring to erotic love that
is ordered to the reception of divine love from Jesus Christ. When erotic
love is not ordered to God it is, writes Benedict XVI, "[a]n intoxicated and
undisciplined *eros*" and consequently is "a fall, a degradation of man." To
be an elevation of man "*eros* needs to be disciplined and purified if it is to
provide not just fleeting pleasure, but a certain foretaste of the pinnacle of
our existence, of that beatitude for which our whole being yearns."[5] The
lovers in the Song of Solomon represent disciplined *eros*. This is evident
in the text indicating that although yearning for union with one another,
the unmarried couple discipline themselves and do not engage in non-
marital sexual activity.

As pointed out by Bergsma and Pitre, despite her desire for her lover,
even expressed in erotic dreams (Song of Solomon 3:1-2; 5:2-3), the
woman retains her virginity: "A garden locked is my sister, my bride, a
garden locked, a fountain sealed (Song of Solomon 4:12 *RSVCE*)." In the
last chapter, the virginity of the woman is again affirmed poetically and

---

    [4] Benedict XVI, "*Encyclical Letter Deus Caritas Est*, no. 7," w2.vatican.va,
http://w2.vatican.va/content/benedict-xvi/en/encyclicals/documents/hf_ben-
xvi_enc_20051225_deus-caritas-est.html.
    [5] Benedict XVI, "*Encyclical Letter Deus Caritas Est*, no. 4," w2.vatican.va.

also assured of being defended: "What shall we do for our sister, on the day when she is spoken for? If she is a wall, we will build upon her a battlement of silver; but if she is a door, we will enclose her with boards of cedar (Song of Solomon 8:8-9 *RSVCE*)." The woman responds to the promise that her virginity, represented by a closed door and wall, by strongly asserting, "I am a wall (Solomon 8:10 *NAB*) .... My vineyard, my very own, is for myself (Song of Solomon 8:11 *RSVCE*)."[6]

---

[6] John Bergsma and Brant Pitre, *A Catholic Introduction to the Bible, Volume I* (San Francisco: Ignatius Press, 2018), Kindle location 14441, 14443.

[7] Gemäldegalerie [Public domain], "The Madonna on a Crescent Moon in Hortus Conclusus, anonymous painter," https://commons.wikimedia.org/wiki/File:15th-century unknown painters - Madonna on a Crescent Moon in Hortus Conclusus - WGA23736.jpg.

The Song of Solomon praises human erotic love that is directed towards marriage, its proper context where sexual intimacy is contained, disciplined, and elevated to God. The perfection of erotic love, though, is only attained in Christ, as Benedict XVI explains:

> God is the absolute and ultimate source of all being; but this universal principle of creation—the *Logos*, primordial reason—is at the same time a lover with all the passion of a true love. Eros is thus supremely ennobled, yet at the same time it is so purified as to become one with agape. We can thus see how the reception of the *Song of Songs* in the canon of sacred Scripture was soon explained by the idea that these love songs ultimately describe God's relation to man and man's relation to God. Thus, the *Song of Songs* became, both in Christian and Jewish literature, a source of mystical knowledge and experience, an expression of the essence of biblical faith: that man can indeed enter into union with God—his primordial aspiration. But this union is no mere fusion, a sinking in the nameless ocean of the Divine; it is a unity which creates love, a unity in which both God and man remain themselves and yet become fully one. As Saint Paul says: "He who is united to the Lord becomes one spirit with him" (1 Cor 6:17).[8]

Section Questions

1. In reference to body language and truth, how does John Paul II interpret the Song of Solomon?

2. In reference to Benedict XVI's writings on Eros and Agape, what does the Song of Solomon teach on giving love, receiving love, and perfection of love?

---

[8] Benedict XVI, "*Encyclical Letter Deus Caritas Est*, no. 10," w2.vatican.va.

Divine Love Interpretation

The Song of Solomon has been interpreted in both Jewish tradition and Christian tradition as spiritually representing the divine love that God, as bridegroom (Isaiah 61:10, 62:5; Jeremiah 7:34, 25:10, 33:11), has for his

---

⁹ Alvesgaspar [CC BY-SA 4.0 (https://creativecommons.org/licenses/by-sa/4.0)], "The Ecstasy of Saint Theresa by Giancarlo Bernini. Church of Santa Maria della Vittoria, Rome," https://commons.wikimedia.org/wiki/File: Ecstasy of Saint Teresa September 2015-2a.jpg.

chosen people, his bride. In Jewish tradition, the bride is Israel and in Catholicism the bride is the new Israel, which includes all people, at least potentially, who have been chosen through Jesus Christ, the bridegroom (Matthew 9:15; John 3:29, 2 Cor. 11:2, Rev. 19:7).

A similar spiritual interpretation in Christianity also identifies the bridegroom with God, with Jesus, but then identifies the bride as an individual believer who yearns to be definitively united with God. Bergsma and Pitre direct our attention to Thérèse of Lisieux and John Paul II who interpreted the Song of Solomon in a mystical, individualized manner. "If I had the time," Thérèse once said to novices she was forming, "I would like to comment on the Song of Songs. I have discovered in this book such profound things about the union of the soul with her beloved."[10] On a resonating note, John Paul II encouraged women Religious: "Your personal journey must be like an original new edition of the famous poem in the Song of Songs."[11]

While acknowledging this mystical interpretation of the Song of Solomon, some Church Fathers cautioned beginners in the spiritual life from meditating too much on this book. Gregory of Nyssa counsels:

> [T]he soul of certain people is not ready to listen [to the Song], let them listen to Moses admonishing us not to dare start climb on the spiritual mountain.... We must, when we want to devote ourselves to contemplation [of the Song], forget thoughts related to marriage...so that, having extinguished all carnal appetites, it will be only through the spirit that our intelligence will simmer lovingly, warmed by the fire

---

[10] Blaise Arminjon, *The Cantata of Love: A Verse by Verse Reading of The Song of Songs*, trans. Nelly Marans (San Francisco: Ignatius Press, 1988), Kindle location 559 of 5603; Bergsma and Pitre, *A Catholic Introduction to the Bible, Volume I*, Kindle location 14101.

[11] Arminjon, *The Cantata of Love*, Kindle location 589 of 5603; Bergsma and Pitre, *A Catholic Introduction to the Bible, Volume I*, Kindle location 14101.

that the Lord has come to bring on earth.[12]

In line with this approach, Alobaidi cautions preachers, and those who accompany or direct people spiritually to be careful when preaching and teaching the mystical dimension of the Song of Solomon since "intimacy

---

[12] Arminjon, *The Cantata of Love,* Kindle location 618 of 5603.

[13] Pompeo Batoni [Public domain], "The Ecstasy of St. Catherine of Siena by Pompeo Batoni," https://commons.wikimedia.org/wiki/File:Pompeo_Batoni_-_The_Ecstasy_of_St_Catherine_of_Siena_-_WGA01501.jpg.

and [the] mystical level is always [deeply] personal" and therefore not a topic that ordinarily can be discussed in public, and when in private with prudence. In addition, since the text may be interpreted in a variety of ways, he recommends presenting to engaged couples the text from the standpoint of human love, and presenting the mystical interpretation when commenting on the Song of Solomon to Religious who are advanced in spirituality. However, when the deeply intimate level of the Song of Solomon is touched upon, including to Religious, holy fear of not intruding hastily into the intimate, divine dimension must be maintained, and if entered then one is to tread lightly.[14]

Section Questions

1. According to the divine love interpretation how is God represented as the bridegroom in the Song of Solomon in Jewish tradition and in Catholic tradition?

2. How specifically did Thérèse of Lisieux interpret the Song of Songs in a divine love interpretive manner?

Liturgical Interpretation

Alobaidi suggests that when first composed, the Song of Solomon was influenced by and possibly even borrowed in part from pagan Canaanite poems that exalted human sexuality, especially sexual fertility. Canaanite liturgical rites often centered on agricultural and animal sexual fertility. In

---

[14] Joseph Alobaidi, class notes and lectures on *Wisdom Literature* (Washington, D.C.: Dominican House of Studies, Spring Semester 2008).

its worship of fertility, the ancient Canaanites held that engaging in sexual acts with a Temple Prostitute was a way to be united to a divine being.

While the Old Testament, especially the Pentateuch, repeatedly rejects nature worship and its associated ritual prostitution, human sexual procreation was understood as holy when expressed in its proper context of marriage and is the way to fulfill the first commandment given by God, the source of life and fertility, "be fruitful and multiple (Genesis 9:7 *RSVCE*)." As Alobaidi explains, the Song of Solomon can be understood as an Israelite response to the disordered, undisciplined erotic liturgy of the Canaanites by presenting disciplined erotic love poetry that is ordered to marriage and through marriage to God, a God of truthful love.[15]

In bringing out the Israelite liturgical interpretation hidden in the text, Bergsma and Pitre ask, "Who would ever compare a woman's neck to a tower, or her hair to goats, or her breasts to gazelles? … The Hebrew imagery used to describe the bride occurs elsewhere in the Bible applied to the city of Jerusalem and the Temple."[16] The following are a few citations that Bergsma and Pitre quote which appear to support their liturgical explanation of bride's strange descriptions.

The verse from 2 Chronicles, "And [Solomon] made the [curtain in the Temple] of blue and purple and crimson fabrics and fine linen. (2 Chron 3:14)" resembles the Song of Solomon, "I am very dark, but comely, O daughters of Jerusalem, like the tents of Kedar, like the curtains of Solomon. (Song 1:5)"[17]

The verse from 1 Kings "[Solomon] built the house of the Forest of Lebanon; . . . upon three rows of cedar pillars, with cedar beams. (1 Kings 7:2)" resembles the following verse from the Song of Solomon, "The scent

---

[15] Alobaidi, class notes and lectures.

[16] John Bergsma and Brant Pitre, *A Catholic Introduction to the Bible, Volume I* (San Francisco: Ignatius Press, 2018), Kindle location 14245.

[17] Bergsma and Pitre, *A Catholic Introduction to the Bible, Volume I*, Kindle location 14463 of 31735.

of your garments is like the scent of Lebanon. (Song 4:11)"[18]

The verse from 2 Chronicles "In front of the house [Solomon] made . . . a hundred pomegranates and put them on chains. (2 Chron 3:15-16)" resembles the following verse from the Song of Solomon, "Your shoots are an orchard of pomegranates with all choicest fruits. (Song 4:13)"[19]

Finally, the verse from Zechariah, "On that day there shall be a fountain opened for . . . inhabitants of Jerusalem. . . . On that day living waters shall flow out from Jerusalem. (Zech 13:1, 14:8)" resembles the following verse from the Song of Solomon "A garden locked is my sister, my bride, . . . a garden fountain, a well of living water. (Song 4:12, 15)."[20]

Pitre additionally cites texts on the bridegroom from the Song of Solomon that parallel texts in other Old Testament books which depict God as Israel's bridegroom.[21]

In continuity with the Jewish liturgical interpretation of the Song of Solomon, some Church Fathers also interpreted the book liturgically but in reference to the Sacraments as an extension of Christ's life through the Church.

Cyril of Jerusalem, observes Blaise Arminjon, eucharistically interprets the desire of the bride to kiss the bridegroom: "Let him kiss me with the kisses of his mouth! (Song of Solomon 1:2 *RSVCE*)." According to Cyril, this passage is fulfilled in Catholicism when the Eucharist is

---

[18] Bergsma and Pitre, *A Catholic Introduction to the Bible, Volume I*, Kindle location 14463 of 31735.

[19] Bergsma and Pitre, *A Catholic Introduction to the Bible, Volume I*, Kindle location 14463 of 31735.

[20] Bergsma and Pitre, *A Catholic Introduction to the Bible, Volume I*, Kindle location 14463 of 31735.

[21] Deuteronomy 6:4-5 with Song of Songs 1:7, 3:1, 2, 3, 4; Psalm 118:24 with Song of Songs 1:4; Psalm 23:1-2 with Song of Songs 1:7; Psalm 19:9-10 with Song of Songs 5:16, Exodus 6:7 with Song of Songs 6:3. Brant Pitre, *Jesus the Bridegroom: The Greatest Love Story Ever Told* (New York: Image, 2014), 22-23.

received. "When the body of Christ will touch your lips," Cyril writes, "then the wish of the Bride will be fulfilled for you: let him kiss me with the kisses of his mouth! The unity of love in the Spirit is then consummated."[22]

Section Question

1. What are various liturgical interpretations of the Song of Songs. Include the following in a specific manner in your response: Temple Prostitution, Idolatry, Woman as Temple, Eucharistic/ Sacramental Interpretation.

---

[22] Blaise Arminjon, *The Cantata of Love: A Verse by Verse Reading of The Song of Songs*, trans. Nelly Marans (San Francisco: Ignatius Press, 1988), Kindle location 758 of 5603.

Wisdom

Introduction

The Book of Wisdom, also known as the Wisdom of Solomon, was originally written not in Hebrew but in Greek and was composed, maintain many Scripture scholars, in Alexandria Egypt sometime between 300 B.C. and the birth of Christ. With respect to Christ, Wisdom functions, writes Bergsma and Pitre, "almost as a kind of 'bridge' between the Old Testament and New Testaments."[2] In this role, Wisdom is the culmination of teaching present in the previous books of Wisdom. In summarizing the teaching of Wisdom in relationship to Solomon, the attributed author, Bergsma and Pitre write, "in Proverbs, he [Solomon] attains the wisdom that leads to temporal success; (2) in Ecclesiastes, he despairs of temporal success because death renders it vain; (3) in the Song, he discovers that love is stronger than death (Song 8:6); (4) in Wisdom, he falls in love with Lady Wisdom and so attains immortality."[3]

When examining the specific content in the book of Wisdom, a logical pattern and structure is not immediately evident, but it can be found. A way Alobaidi divides the book is as follows: Wisdom and Judgment (Wisdom 1:1-5:23), The Wisdom of Solomon for Rulers of the Nations (Wisdom 6:1-9:18), and Wisdom in Salvation History (Wisdom 10:1-19:22).[4]

Section Questions

1. When was the book of Wisdom written and in what language?

2. How do Bergsma and Pitre explain the progression of the following Wisdom books as reflected in Solomon maturing as he

---

[2] John Bergsma and Brant Pitre, *A Catholic Introduction to the Bible, Volume I* (San Francisco: Ignatius Press, 2018), Kindle location 15001 of 31735.

[3] Bergsma and Pitre, *A Catholic Introduction to the Bible, Volume I,* Kindle location 14678 of 31735.

[4] Joseph Alobaidi, class notes and lectures on *Wisdom Literature* (Washington, D.C.: Dominican House of Studies, Spring Semester 2008).

ages: Proverbs, Ecclesiastes, Song of Songs, Wisdom. Include the following in your response: success, vanity, death, immortality.

Wisdom and Judgment (1:1-5:23)

The first section on judgment opens by encouraging the practice of goodness and the avoidance of evil: "Love righteousness...for perverse thoughts separate men from God, and when his power is tested, it convicts the foolish (Wisdom 1:1-3 *RSVCE*)." After describing the rationalizations the wicked use to justify their evil ways (chapter two), chapter three through five teaches that the wicked will be judged by God, "the ungodly will be punished as their reasoning deserves (Wisdom 3:10 *RSVCE*)" while the righteous "will receive great good, because God tested them and found

---

[5] "Judgment of Solomon, an engraving by Gustave Doré (19 century)," https://commons.wikimedia.org/wiki/File:Judgement_of_Solomon.jpg.

them worthy of himself (Wisdom 3:5 *RSVCE*)."

Although Christianity emphasizes love and mercy, it does not do so by denying Wisdom's teaching on God as the ultimate judge. As Benedict XVI clearly states, "Let us not forget, however, that the God of reason and of love is also the Judge of the world and of mankind—the guarantor of justice, to whom men must render an accounting. Given the temptations to power, it is a fundamental obligation to keep in mind the truth about the Judgment: every one of us must someday give an account. There is a justice that is not abolished by love."[6]

Benedict XVI encourages priests when they preach the Good News of Jesus Christ not to omit proclaiming that God "enters into history to do justice."

[O]ne aspect of the preaching Jesus, which is often omitted today: The proclamation of the Kingdom of God is the proclamation of the God present, the God that knows us, listen to us; the God that enters into history to do justice. Therefore, this preaching is also the proclamation of justice, the proclamation of our responsibility.

Man cannot do or avoid doing what he wants to. He will be judged. He must account for things. This certitude is of value both for the powerful as well as the simple ones. Where this is honored, the limitations of every power in this world are traced. God renders justice, and only he may ultimately do this.[7]

---

[6] Joseph Ratzinger, *Europe, Today and Tomorrow: Addressing the Fundamental Issues*, trans. J. Miller (San Francisco: Ignatius Press, 2007), 97-98.

[7] Joseph Cardinal Ratzinger, "Address to Catechists and Religion Teachers, Jubilee of Catechists, 12 December 2000," Piercedhearts.org https://www.piercedhearts.org/benedict_xvi/Cardinal%20Ratzinger/new_evangelization.htm

In relating the justice of God to mercy, Pope Francis comments that justice and mercy:

> are not two contradictory realities, but two dimensions of a single reality that unfolds progressively until it culminates in the fullness of love. ... Mercy is not opposed to justice but rather expresses God's way of reaching out to the sinner, offering him a new chance to look at himself, convert, and believe. ... God goes beyond justice with his mercy and forgiveness. Yet this does not mean that justice should be devalued or rendered superfluous. On the contrary: anyone who makes a mistake must pay the price. ...God's justice is his mercy given to everyone as a grace that flows from the death and resurrection of Jesus Christ. Thus, the Cross of Christ is God's judgement on all of us and on the whole world, because through it he offers us the certitude of love and new life.[8]

Reaching back to the medieval age, the scholastic Thomas Aquinas, teaching on the relationship of justice and mercy, resonates with Pope Francis's teaching that justice and mercy "are two dimensions of a single reality." If only one dimension of this reality is stressed, then either justice or mercy is fictionalized, as a coin with only one side exists in the imagination alone. In the words of Aquinas, "justice without mercy is cruelty, while mercy without justice is the mother of destruction. Therefore, it is necessary for the two to be joined, as it says in Proverbs (3:3): 'Let not mercy and truth forsake you'; 'Mercy and truth will meet'

---

[8] Pope Francis, "Misericordiae Vultus, Bull of Indiction of the Extraordinary Jubilee of Mercy, no. 20-21," w2.vatican.va, http://w2.vatican.va/content/francesco/en/apost_letters/documents/papa-francesco_bolla_20150411_misericordiae-vultus.html.

(Ps 85:10)."[9]

The cited texts from the Judaism of the Old Testament, which Catholicism builds upon and fulfills, indicate that God is both merciful and just. Representing Judaism's perspective, Abba Hillel Silver writes:

> Judaism teaches that God is both loving, forgiving and just. In addition, justice is not an antonym for love; hate is. Finally, when the bible mentions the attributes of God his just and loving qualities are balanced with a bias towards love. According to the Rabbis God's two titles of YHVH and Elohim designate God as merciful and just. "In the day that the Lord God –YHVH Elohim – made earth and heaven," a Rabbi said: "This may be compared to a king who had some empty glasses. The king said: "If I pour hot water into them they will crack; if I pour ice-cold water into them they will also crack!" What did the king do? He mixed the hot and cold water together and poured it into them and they did not crack. Even so did the Holy One, bless be He, say: "If I create the world on the basis of the attribute of mercy alone, the world's sins will greatly multiply. If I create it on the basis of the attribute of justice alone, how could the world endure? I will therefore create it with both the attributes of mercy and justice, and it may endure!" (Gen R. 12:15)[10]

The understanding of how God is just to human beings underwent a process of development that Catholics believe is fulfilled in Jesus, Who is the fullness of Revelation. Before the time the book of Wisdom was written, it was not clear as to how God rewards the just and punishes the wicked. This lack of clarity was due to an undeveloped sense of what

---

[9] Thomas Aquinas, "Super Evangelium S. Matthaei lectura, chapter 5, lectio 2," https://isidore.co/aquinas/SSMatthew.htm#5.

[10] Abba Hillel Silver, *Where Judaism Differs* (New York: Collier Books, 1989), 109.

happens to human beings after they die. Unlike the earlier Old Testament books, the book of Wisdom clearly teaches that the soul is immortal and, as a consequence, that those righteous people who suffer in this present world will one day in the next life receive their just reward from God:

> The righteous man who has died will condemn the ungodly who are living, and youth that is quickly perfected will condemn the prolonged old age of the unrighteous man. For they will see the end of the wise man, and will not understand what the Lord purposed for him, and for what he kept him safe. They will see, and will have contempt for him, but the Lord will laugh them to scorn. After this they will become dishonored corpses, and an outrage among the dead for ever (Wisdom 4:17-18 *RSVCE*).

The Jewish people, explains Alobaidi, gradually came to the awareness of the soul's immortality. This gradual revelation took place by God's working providentially through the Greek culture. At the time the book of Wisdom was being written, Greek culture was the dominant culture as evident by the book's being written in Greek in the city of Alexandria, named after the Macedonian conqueror, Alexander the Great, who advanced Hellenistic (Greek) culture throughout his empire. The Jewish encounter with the Greek Platonic concept of the immaterial, eternal nature of the soul helped to also deepen the Jewish understanding of justice. Unlike earlier books, the book of Wisdom with its Greek influence clearly teaches that although justice may not be evident in this life it will be in the next life.[11]

---

[11] Alobaidi, class notes and lectures.

Section Questions

1. With respect to dimensions, how does Pope Francis describe justice and mercy, and how specifically is this similar to Aquinas's explanation?

2. By clearly affirming the immortality of the soul, how did the book of Wisdom deepen the Old Testament understanding of divine justice?

---

[12] Raphael [Public domain], "Plato (left) and Aristotle (right) a detail of The School of Athens, a fresco by Raphael. Aristotle gestures to the earth while holding a copy of his Nicomachean Ethics in his hand. Plato holds his Timaeus and gestures to the heavens," https://commons.wikimedia.org/wiki/File:Sanzio_01_Plato_Aristotle.jpg.

The Wisdom of Solomon for Rulers of the Nations (Wisdom 6:1-9:18)

This section opens with Solomon's teaching wisdom to all rulers, Gentile or Jewish, "Listen therefore, O kings, and understand; learn, O judges of the ends of the earth (Wisdom 6:1 *RSVCE*)." As Pope Francis simply defines, "wisdom … is seeing with God's eyes, listening with God's ears, loving with God's heart, judging things with Gods' judgment."[13] Solomon in the book of Wisdom chapter 7 similarly describes wisdom as a gift from God which enables one to see the world through the eyes and heart of God, "I prayed, and understanding was given me; I called upon God, and the spirit of wisdom came to me (Wisdom 7:7 *RSVCE*)."

---

[13] Francis, "The Gift of Wisdom: Pope Francis Begins Series of Talks on the Gifts of the Holy Spirit," catholic.org, https://www.catholic.org/news/international/europe/story.php?id=54889.

[14] Julius Schnorr von Carolsfeld [Public domain], "Solomon and Lady Wisdom by Julius Schnorr von Karolsfeld, 1860," https://commons.wikimedia.org/wiki/File:Schnorr_von_Carolsfeld_Bibel_in_Bildern_1860_138.png.

The book of Wisdom not only defines wisdom with respect to how God understands the world but also in relationship to how Solomon is to act in accordance with this divine perception, "For she knows and understands all things, and she will guide me wisely in my actions and guard me with her glory. Then my works will be acceptable, and I shall judge thy people justly, and shall be worthy of the throne of my father. For what man can learn the counsel of God? Or who can discern what the Lord wills? (Wisdom 9:11-13 *RSVCE*)."

Providentially, the presentation of wisdom as encompassing both knowledge, knowing the world through God's understanding, and practice, acting in accordance with this divine knowledge, prepared for the incarnation when the uncreated wisdom of the father was born in Bethlehem. In the words of Benedict XVI, this "unique narrowing of the concept of wisdom" affected how the Jewish people at the time of Jesus understood an expert of Torah: "Thus it is not the recognized Torah expert who is considered wise but he in whom knowing and doing have become one."[15] Jesus fulfills this heavenly and practical knowledge as wisdom in the flesh in whom knowing truth and doing truth are perfectly united. Reflecting this practical definition of wisdom inherited from the Old Testament and fulfilled in Jesus Christ, St. Augustine, continues Benedict XVI, relates wisdom to the beatitude of Matthew's gospel, "Blessed are the peacemakers (Matthew 5:9 *RSVCE*)." Benedict XVI comments:

> At first glance, it may seem surprising that wisdom is not linked to the vision of God, to the promise that the pure of heart shall see God. Instead, it is very practical in its orientation, very earthbound: the work of peace. But it is precisely because wisdom is a penetrating of the depths, an entering into God's own perspective, into his Spirit, that

---

[15] Joseph Ratzinger, *Principles of Catholic Theology: Building Stones for a Fundamental Theology*, trans. M.F. McCarthy (San Francisco: Ignatius Press, 1987), 359-364.

it is not something merely private and interior but a sharing in the work of the Messiah: My peace I give you.[16]

The voice of Solomon in the second section of the book of wisdom encourages kings to seek this practical knowledge called wisdom in which eternally truthful knowledge informs loving action. If the definition of a king is solely in a political sense, then it is difficult to see how Solomon's teachings apply to the kings of today since the few remaining kings in the world typically only have symbolic roles. If, though, the definition of king is broadened to include what and who is most influential today, then the teaching is easily applicable. In applying this teaching to scientific reasoning, which tends to limit reason to clear, distinct, exact knowledge while relating all other ways of knowing to what is unreasonable and irrational, Benedict XVI warns that since human behavior cannot be exactly predicted or defined, human beings themselves are then automatically also relegated to the irrational realm.

Once this takes place, the only way to govern is by commands that do not appeal to reason but instead to fear. In governing by fear rather than reason, authorities command individuals to comply with the threat of punishment for failure to comply. The way of governing that this second section of the book of Wisdom educates rulers in is by reason that is preceded by a desire for divine knowledge and is shaped by ruling through the gift of knowledge given by God. This divinely given knowledge, known as wisdom, can never be exactly grasped with precision in the same way that knowledge that is acquired by the empirical sciences is. In addition, wisdom relates not only to the intellect but also to the will since rulers are called to act in an appropriate way determined by the received divine knowledge.[17]

---

[16] Ratzinger, *Principles of Catholic Theology*, 359-364.
[17] Ratzinger, *Principles of Catholic Theology*, 359-364.

Section Questions

1. What gift did Solomon prefer "to scepters and thrones"?

2. How is wisdom **not** presented as purely speculative, theoretical knowledge? In addition, how does Jesus's birth fulfill this understanding of wisdom?

Wisdom in Salvation History (Wisdom 10:1-19:22)

The third section of the book of Wisdom approaches salvation history from a wisdom perspective. A main theme in this section is on the foolishness of idolatry and the wisdom of right worship of God. The two main forms of idolatry identified in chapters thirteen and fourteen are nature worship and the worship of objects made by humans.

The worship of nature is followed by a desire to imitate nature in a manner that is disordered since human beings are to imitate God more than imitating nature. This is particularly the case in how human beings are to love. Nature worship and the practical effects of this idolatry on how human love is expressed is still relevant for today. Imitating how rams love ewes or bulls love cows is disordered since men and women are made in the image and likeness of God not in the image and likeness of any creatures. Therefore, how we love, including how we give and receive love is to be informed primarily by how God loves as Revelation teaches. In addition, the worship of objects made by human hands is also still relevant in our fast pace world where work is idolized by being perceived as the most essential aspect in people's lives.

When work is glorified, love of neighbor and love of God easily become sacrificed for the sake of the idol of work. For the sake of work, and not out of love of God and neighbor, people race around, observes Ron Rolheiser, "blind…to the needs of others." Research done at Princeton University, writes Rolheiser, demonstrates a relationship between haste and ignoring the needs of our neighbors:

> In 1970, Princeton University did some research with seminary students to determine whether being committed to helping others in fact made a real difference in a practical situation. They set up this scenario: They would interview a seminarian in an office and, as the interview was ending, ask that seminarian to immediately walk over to a designated classroom across the campus to give a talk. But they always put a tight timeline between when the interview ended and when the seminarian was supposed to appear in the classroom, forcing the seminarian to hurry. On the way to the talk, each seminarian encountered an actor playing a distressed person (akin to the Good Samaritan scene in the gospels). The test was to see whether or not the seminarian would stop and help. What was the result?

One would guess that, being seminarians committed to service, these individuals might be more likely to stop than most other people. But that wasn't the case. Being seminarians seemed to have no effect on their behavior in this situation. Only one thing did: They were prone to stop and help or to not stop and help mostly on the basis of whether they were in a hurry or not. If they were pressured for time, they didn't stop; if they were not pressured for time, they were more likely to stop.[18]

When we allow ourselves to be overly absorbed by work, we become blind to the needs of those around us. May we repent from our tendency to idolize work. In an English translation of the Bible, the word repent is

---

[18] Ron Rolheiser, "Always In a Hurry," June 2, 2013, ronrolheiser.com, http://ronrolheiser.com/always-in-a-hurry/#.WEQX93e-Ki5, (accessed Dec. 4, 2016).

often a translation of the Greek word *metanoia* (μετάνοια, ας, ἡ). *Metanoia* (μετάνοια, ας, ἡ) is based on the word *meta* meaning, beyond or above and *noús*, meaning mind.[19] In reference to Henri Nouwen, Ron Rolheiser contrasts the open-minded repentance of metanoia with closed-mindedness of paranoia.[20] Paranoia literally means in Greek by the side of the mind. Paranoid people, in other words, do not allow themselves to transcend the problems of this world. This state of mind causes the paranoid to be anxious, humorless, and devoid of charity since they are overly absorbed by the cares of this world. Those open to repentance (*metanoia*) rise above the problems of this world and by so doing they are receptive to being formed by God's peaceful ways as they, in the words of Dietrich Von Hildebrand, stand firm in God, meaning a "standing-firm against all tendencies to change that come from below and a sensitive receptivity to every change that would mold us from above."[21]

Resisting being conformed solely to nature while remaining open to heavenly transformation necessarily will affect how human sexuality is expressed. In recognition of this connection between worship of nature and how human sexuality is expressed, the book of Wisdom argues that idolatry of nature leads to "confusion over what is good, forgetfulness of favors, pollution of souls, sex perversion, disorder in marriage, adultery, and debauchery. For the worship of idols not to be named is the beginning and cause and end of every evil (Wisdom of Solomon 14:26-27 *RSVCE*)." With that said, as Alobaidi points out, if nature is contemplated and not

---

[19] "Strong's 3326. Meta," biblehub.com, https://biblehub.com/greek/3326.htm; "Strong's 3539. Noéo," biblehub.com, https://biblehub.com/greek/3539.htm.

[20] Ron Rolheiser, "From Paranoia to Metanoia," September 12, 2016, ronrolheiser.com, http://ronrolheiser.com/from-paranoia-to-metanoia/#.W2TM-C2ZNcB.

[21] Joseph Ratzinger, *Principles of Catholic Theology: Building Stones for a Fundamental Theology*, trans. M.F. McCarthy (San Francisco: Ignatius Press, 1987), 62.

idolized as our final end, then through the contemplation of nature one is able to encounter God and grow in wisdom by allowing God to reach through nature and transform us according to his divine ways.[22]

For example, the patience exhibited in certain natural processes can instruct us on the patience of God and what it means to be patient like God especially with respect to chastity. Ron Rolheiser compares impatient unchaste ways to the attempt to speed up the process of a moth slowly emerging by lighting a candle underneath the cocoon. By so doing the moth will be destroyed or at least stunted in growth. Similarly, states Rolheiser:

Properly understood, chastity is precisely a question of having the patience to bear the tension of the interminable slowness of things. To

---

[22] Alobaidi, class notes and lectures.

[23] Museo Nazionale di Capodimonte [Public domain], "Pieter Brueghel, The parable of the blind (1568)," https://commons.wikimedia.org/wiki/File:%D0%9F%D1%80%D0%B8%D1%82%D1%87%D0%B0_%D0%BE_%D1%81%D0%BB%D0%B5%D0%BF%D1%8B%D1%85.jpeg.

be chaste is to not prematurely force things so that everybody and everything, each within its own unique rhythm is properly respected.

... To be chaste is to stand before reality, everything and everybody, and fully respect the proper contours and rhythm of things. To be chaste then means to let things unfold as they should. Thus it means, among many other things, to not open our gifts before Christmas, to not rush our own or our children's growth, to not experience things for which we aren't ready, to not lose patience in life or in sex because there is tension, to not violate someone else's beauty and sexuality, to not apply a candle to a moth emerging from its cocoon because we're in a hurry, and to not sleep with the bride before the wedding.

To be chaste is to let gift be gift. Biblically, to be chaste is to have our shoes off before the burning bush. Chastity is reverence and respect. All irreverence and disrespect is the antithesis of chastity. Chastity as a practical virtue is then predicated on two things: Patience and the capacity to carry tension.

Patience is basically synonymous with chastity. To fully respect others and the proper order of things means to be patient. Something can be wrong for no other reason that that it is premature. To do anything too quickly, whether that be growing up, or having sex, does what applying extra heat does to the process of metamorphosis. It leaves us with damaged wings.

...

The capacity to carry tension is too an integral part of chastity. To properly respect others, to have the patience to not act prematurely, requires that we be willing and able to carry tension and to carry it for a long time, perhaps even for a lifetime. To wait in tension, in incompleteness, in longing, in frustration, in inconsummation, and in helplessness in the face of the interminable slowness of things, especially in the face of how slow love and justice seem to appear in our lives, is to practice chastity.

When Jesus sweated blood in the Garden of Gethsemane he was practicing chastity; just as when Mary stood under the cross, unable to stop its senselessness and unable even to protest Jesus' innocence, she too was practicing chastity. Unless we are willing to carry tension, in the same way, we will, precisely, never wait for the wedding night.

Chastity's challenge reads this way: Never short-circuit the process of metamorphosis. Whether you are dealing with sex or with life in general, wait for the wedding night for the consummation. [24]

Section Questions

1. What are the two main forms of idolatry that are condemned in Wisdom chapters thirteen and fourteen?

2. Why does Wisdom teach that "worship of idols ... is the beginning and cause and end of every evil (Wisdom14:27)." In your response, include the following: Metanoia, Love Formed from what is Below, Love Formed what is Above.

---

[24] Ron Rolheiser, "Chastity's Challenge," December 16, 1998, ronrolheiser.com, http://ronrolheiser.com/chastitys-challenge/#.XVl3gC2ZNuV

---

[25] "Patience, engraving by Hans Sebald Beham, 1540," enwikipedia.org, https://en.wikipedia.org/wiki/Patience#/media/File:Pacientia_or_Patience.jpg.

Sirach

Introduction

The book of Sirach was originally written in Hebrew by Ben Sira "son of Sirach (Sirach 50:27 *RSVCE*)" and translated into Greek by his

---

[1] Workshop of Jörg Breu the Younger [Public domain], "Illustration of the high priest Jesus Sirach in the *Secret Book of Honour of the Fugger*, 1545–1549," https://commons.wikimedia.org/wiki/File:Fugger_Ehrenbuch_001.jpg.

grandson. In reference to the original text of his "grandfather," the grandson tells the reader in the prologue: "For what was originally expressed in Hebrew does not have exactly the same sense when translated into another language (Sirach Prologue, *RSVCE*)." Fragments of the original text in Hebrew were found in Qumran, Masada, and in Geniza, Cairo.[2]

Ben Sira describes his writing as "the last on watch (Sirach 33:16 *RSVCE*)" of the Wisdom Literature tradition: "I was like one who gleans after the grape-gatherers; by the blessing of the Lord I excelled…I have not labored for myself alone, but for all who seek instruction (Sirach 33:16-17 *RSVCE*)." In the book, Ben Sira repeatedly offers instruction for social harmony. For this reason, one Greek title of the book is Ecclesiasticus. The diminutive word of the Greek word for Church indicates, according to Bergsma and Pitre, that it was seen as "the Church's little book."[3] The wisdom that this "little book" teaches, writes Alobaidi, "is … a wisdom that helps to maintain a stable biblical social order where leaders and institutions are respected."[4]

The practical teachings on maintaining social harmony are a way Sirach serves as a bridge to the New Testament of Jesus Christ, who unlike Barabbas, did not set out to disrupt the social order but rather lived a life of patient obedience to his heavenly Father's will. His Father's will was at times manifested through the authorities of this world. As Romans teaches, "there is no authority except from God, and those what exist have been instituted by God (Romans 13:1 *RSVCE*)." Consequently, all are, teaches Romans, to "be subject to the governing authorities (Romans 13:1 *RSVCE*)." Similarly, St. Peter teaches, "Be subject for the Lord's sake to

---

[2] Joseph Alobaidi, class notes and lectures on *Wisdom Literature* (Washington, D.C.: Dominican House of Studies, Spring Semester 2008).

[3] John Bergsma and Brant Pitre, *A Catholic Introduction to the Bible, Volume I* (San Francisco: Ignatius Press, 2018), Kindle location 15119 of 31735.

[4] Alobaidi, class notes and lectures.

every human institution, whether it be to the emperor as supreme, or to governors … Honor all men. Love the brotherhood. Fear God. Honor the emperor (1 Peter 2:13-17 *RSVCE*)."[5]

We will reflect on the Sirach teaching on social order by surveying this theme through the three basic sections of Sirach identified by Bergsma and Pitre: "first collection of instruction," "second collection of instruction," and a "review of sacred history."

---

[5] Joseph Ratzinger, *Church, Ecumenism and Politics: New Endeavors in Ecclesiology* (San Francisco: Ignatius Press, 2008), 167.

[6] "Untitled, known in English as The Arnolfini Portrait, The Arnolfini Wedding, The Arnolfini Marriage, The Arnolfini Double Portrait, or Portrait of Giovanni Arnolfini and his Wife," https://en.wikipedia.org/wiki/File:Van_Eyck_-_Arnolfini_Portrait.jpg#file.

Section Questions

1. With respect to the Church, what is the meaning of the alternative title Ecclesiasticus?

First Collection of Wisdom Teaching (Sirach 1-23)

The first collection begins with a chapter praising wisdom. In the praise, the fear of the Lord is described as "the beginning of wisdom." Fear of the Lord is also identified as an originating reality that "is created with the faithful in the womb (Sirach 1:14 *RSVCE*)." This fear of the Lord is connected to keeping the commandments (1:26), which ensures a proper, God-centered social order.

In grounding proper social order in God, the following chapter, chapter two, explains how to relate to God: patiently, in fear, trusting in divine mercy, and with love. Chapters three through six then shift the focus from relating to God to relating more horizontally to our fellow human beings, beginning with parents. This part emphasizes maintaining harmony and order by being meek, humble, patient, and coming to the aid of those on the fringes of societal order: "do not…delay your gift to a beggar. Do not reject an afflicted suppliant, nor turn your face away from the poor (Sirach 4:3-4 *RSVCE*)." Echoing the social laws of Exodus, the section affirms, points out Bergsma and Pitre, the need to protect the vulnerable of society especially the stranger, the widow, and the orphan (Exodus 22:21-23).[7]

Chapters seven through nine advise on how to relate to a variety of people including the powerful, friends, servants, laborers, children, priests, the poor, the rich, the ill-bred, the aged, the foolish, the angry, the stranger,

---

[7] Bergsma and Pitre, *A Catholic Introduction to the Bible, Volume I,* Kindle location 15598 of 31735.

one's wife, other men's wives, loose women, virgins, and prostitutes. Chapters ten through twenty-three provide a wide range of wisdom teaching. Topics touched upon include ruling, pride, humility, honor, true friends and false friends, use of wealth, choosing properly, punishment of sin, divine justice, repentance, generosity, caution, true wisdom and the false wisdom of worldly cleverness, speech and silence, self-control, the addictive nature and misery of sexual sins.

One topic that, unless it is carefully interpreted, is rightly disturbing is the role of women. There is even one verse that even asserts that "the birth of a daughter is a loss (Sirach 22:3 *RSVCE*)." Bergsma and Pitre point out that this troubling verse is not as problematic when seen in its context which uses a "Hebrew poetic device known as *synonymous parallelism*, in which parallel lines mutually illuminate the meaning of other lines."[8] They continue:

When the line is read in its poetic context, it becomes very clear that Sirach is not referring to the birth of any daughter, but the birth of a shameful daughter, since in the very next verse he praises a sensible daughter: It is a disgrace to be the father of an undisciplined son, and the birth of a[n undisciplined] daughter is a loss. A sensible daughter obtains her husband, but one who acts shamefully brings grief to her father. (Sir 22:3-4) Taken as a whole, then, the passage seems to be contrasting unsensible daughters with sensible ones—not declaring that all daughters are worthless.[9]

Even so, strictly speaking, the birth of any female or male baby is a blessing since all are equally adopted children of our Heavenly Father.

---

[8] Bergsma and Pitre, *A Catholic Introduction to the Bible, Volume I*, Kindle location 15329 of 31735.

[9] Bergsma and Pitre, *A Catholic Introduction to the Bible, Volume I*, Kindle location 15481 of 31735.

Another similarly problematic verse that Bergsma and Pitre strive to carefully interpret in its historical context is, "Better is the wickedness of a man than a woman who does good (Sirach 42:14 *RSVCE*)." This verse, observe Bergsma and Pitre, is stated within the context of warning married men from forming disordered attachments with women other than their wives which are tantamount to, as Proverbs teaches, carrying fire in one's bosom and expecting one's clothes not to be burned or walking on burning coals and expecting not to be burned (Proverbs 6:27-28). In some circumstances, counsels Sirach, it is safer for a married man to relate to a wicked man whom they are not unduly attracted to than to a good woman whom they may be very attracted to and this attraction could lead to the kindling of a fire that burns both the man and the good woman, destroying both.[10]

---

[10] Bergsma and Pitre, *A Catholic Introduction to the Bible, Volume I,* Kindle location 15467 of 31735.

[11] Frederick Goodall [Public domain], "Frederick Goodall's Passionate Encounter," https://commons.wikimedia.org/wiki/File:Frederick_Goodall_RA_-_Passionate_encounter.jpg.

Section Questions

1. According to Sirach, "the birth of a daughter is a loss (Sirach 22:3 *RSVCE*)." In reference to synonymous parallelism, how do Bergsma and Pitre explain this verse in relationship to its context?

2. According to Sirach, "Better is the wickedness of a man than a woman who does good (Sirach 42:14 *RSVCE*)." According to Bergsma and Pitre, what is the immediate context of this verse that allows for an interpretation that is less troubling?

Second Collection of Wisdom Teaching (Sirach 24-43)

Like the first section, the second section begins by praising wisdom (chapter 24). Chapters 25-43 then provide various sets of wisdom teachings on a number of themes including: marital advice, wise and foolish speech, loyalty to friends and betrayal, resentment, quarrelling, slander, order at home, relations with neighbors, hospitality, disciplining of children, moderation, humility when in positions of prominence, just wages, fasting, prayer, divine justice, true and false counselors, medical profession and other professions, joys and sorrows of life, wisdom as reflected in creation.

These teachings on wisdom do not necessarily carry over into Christianity without modification. Rather, borrowing words from Benedict XVI, Sirach's Old Testament teaching "continues to live in the New Testament" but in a transformed sense.[12] An example is Ephesians' teaching that when disciplining their children fathers should not "provoke

---

[12] Benedict XVI, *Dogma and Preaching: Applying Christian Doctrine to Daily Life*, trans. Michael J. Miller (San Francisco: Ignatius Press, 2011), 252-253.

your children to anger (Ephesians 6:4 *RSVCE*)." This New Testament teaching, comment Bergsma and Pitre, is a merciful development of Sirach's instruction: "He who loves his son will whip him often.... Discipline your son and take pains with him, that you may not be offended by his shamelessness (Sirach 30:1, 13 RSVCE)."[13]

Another example of Sirach's wisdom that is further developed, Bergsma and Pitre note, is Sirach's teaching on work as a form of prayer. Laborers are to "rely upon their hands, and each is skillful in his own work. Without them a city cannot be established.... But they keep stable the fabric of the world, and their prayer is in the practice of their trade (Sirach 38:31, 34 *RSVCE*)."[14] Echoing this wisdom, Pope John Paul II in his encyclical letter on work, *Laborem Exercens*, writes, "Let the Christian who listens to the word of the living God, uniting work with prayer, know the place that his work has not only in *earthly progress* but also in *the development of the Kingdom of God,* to which we are all called through the power of the Holy Spirit and through the word of the Gospel."[15] In continuation with this wisdom, Saint Josemaría Escrivá stresses, "Persevere in the exact fulfillment of the obligations of the moment. That work – humble, monotonous, small – is prayer expressed in action that prepares you to receive the grace of the other work – great and wide and deep – of which you dream."[16]

---

[13] Bergsma and Pitre, *A Catholic Introduction to the Bible, Volume I,* Kindle location 15329 of 31735.

[14] Bergsma and Pitre, *A Catholic Introduction to the Bible, Volume I,* Kindle location 15367 of 31735.

[15] John Paul II, *Laborem Exercens,* 1981, w2.vatican.va, http://w2.vatican.va/content/john-paul-ii/en/encyclicals/documents/hf_jp-ii_enc_14091981_laborem-exercens.html, 27.

[16] Josemaría Escrivá, *The Way,* trans. Fundación Studium (New York: Doubleday, 1982), 143.

Section Question

1. How does Ephesians 6:4 specifically modify the teaching of Sirach
   30:1 "He who loves his son will whip him often.... Discipline your
   son and take pains with him, that you may not be offended by his
   shamelessness (Sirach 30:1, 13)."

Wisdom in Salvation History (44-50)

The third section sweeps through salvation history. It begins by
praising key people who live on in the memory of others in contrast with
others "who have no memorial, who have perished as though they had not
lived; they have become as though they had not been born (Sirach 44:9
RSVCE)." In the Resurrection of Jesus, the New Testament strongly
affirms that life after death is not limited to memories of subsequent
generations but rather is a personal reality that is a continuation and
fulfillment of the life that passed.[17]

The prominent people highlighted by Sirach include the following:
Enoch, Noah, Abraham, Isaac, Jacob, Moses, Aaron, Phinehas, Joshua,
Caleb, Judges, Samuel, Nathan, David, Solomon, Elijah, Elisha, Hezekiah,
Isaiah, Josiah, Jeremiah, Ezekiel, 12 Prophets, Zerubbabel, Joshua,
Nehemiah, Simon Son of Onias.

---

[17] Alobaidi, class notes and lectures.

Images of Wisdom Literature by Gustav Doré

Courtesy of Wikimedia Commons

Job Hearing of his Ruin

Job and his Friends

King Solomon in All His Glory

King Solomon Receiving the Queen of Sheba

The Judgment of Solomon

The Folly of Human Conceits

The Wise Men Guided by the Star

Christ in the Synagogue

Christ Mocked

The Erection of the Cross

The Resurrection

www.ingramcontent.com/pod-product-compliance
Lightning Source LLC
Chambersburg PA
CBHW072353090426
42741CB00012B/3022